Martin Vaughn-James

THE CAGE

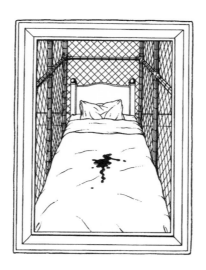

Coach House Books

This book was commenced in January 1972 in Toronto and completed
there in February 1974. The major part of the work was done in Paris
during 1972 and 73.

Originally printed in an edition of 1,500 copies at the Coach House
Press in Toronto in 1975.

Issued in French in 2006 by Les impressions nouvelles and mécanique
générale / Les 400 coups

LIBRARY AND ARCHIVES CANADA CATALOGUING IN PUBLICATION

Vaughn-James, Martin, 1943-2009, artist
     The cage / written and illustrated by Martin Vaughn-James ;
with an introduction by Seth. -- 2nd edition.

ISBN 978-1-55245-287-5 (pbk.)

    1. Graphic novels. I. Title.

PN6733.V38C35 2013   741.5'971   C2013-904093-5

Introduction

Man Fears Time, But Time Fears Only The Pyramids

An appreciation by Seth

I first encountered Martin Vaughn-James's work sometime back in the late eighties at a (sadly, vanished) independent bookstore, This Ain't the Rosedale Library. I was a frequent enough patron for co-owner Charlie Huisken to have known I was a cartoonist, because I recall him excitedly cornering me one day to let me know he'd acquired a stack of first-edition hardcovers of *The Cage* and *The Projector*. I had no idea what he was talking about, but from his tone of voice I gathered that a cultured person *would* know about such things and so I played along. I bought both books, though neither of them was particularly to my taste. Back then (and today, still) I tended to favour a fluid line in drawing that is easily recognized as coming from the commercial cartooning of the early twentieth century – the kind of line the cartoonist of the old *New Yorker* drew with. I am deeply drawn to the simplicity and boldness found in the comics of Hergé or Charles Schulz: a slick, sensual line that has spontaneity and evidence of the human hand in it. The drawings inside Vaughn-James's books looked rather clinical. Photo-realistic even. To me these books had the appearance more of a manual of diagrams than of comics I loved; they were almost the direct opposite of the comics I was drawn to. I doubted these were my cup of tea. Yes, the oddness of the content was intriguing, but truthfully I was more swayed by Charlie's implication that I would be a fool to pass them up.

You're likely expecting to read that when I got home and read them, I fell deeply in love with both books, rushing back to thank

Charlie for changing my life by exposing me to the light of a lost genius. But that is certainly not the case. I didn't fall in love with them; in fact, I was totally perplexed by them. I don't think I initially liked these books *at all*. I found them cold and impenetrable – maybe even off-putting.

Yet they weren't so cold, off-putting and impenetrable that I didn't continue thinking about them. Honestly, I couldn't make heads nor tails of them and yet I was quite sure that these books were more than just some old 'hippy psychedelia.' There was a clear seriousness of purpose about the books that kept me returning to them. And, being the collector type that I am, I even tracked down the rest of Vaughn-James's work to study. It was all interesting, and as expected, it was all perplexing. He's not an easy artist to like. He asks an awful lot of the reader. But I stuck with him and in time came to recognize that *The Cage* was the work I most admired of him – his masterpiece.

I don't use the word 'masterpiece' lightly. I think *The Cage* is a masterpiece of comic art. Published in 1975, it is a visionary graphic novel, far ahead of its time – so far ahead of its time that it was ages before that awkward term had even come into popular usage. True, an art comic book wasn't completely unprecedented; *The Cage* emerges, in some ways, from the underground comics of the late sixties and seventies. But it is so utterly unique that it is barely recognizable as a part of that movement – I certainly never thought of Martin Vaughn-James's work as having anything to do with Robert Crumb or Gilbert Shelton or the like. The underground connection is definitely there, but probably more as spark of inspiration than a direct influence.

I'm not sure if I considered it a 'comic book' when I first read it. It doesn't have the appearance of a comic. There are no word balloons, no characters, the drawing is diagrammatic rather than expressive – it doesn't even have more than one panel per page. If it were the only book he'd ever produced I might be more likely to think he'd patterned it on a children's picture book. It is only when you look at Vaughn-James's full body of work that it becomes obvious that *The Cage* is definitely a comic book. His previous 'graphic novels,' *Elephant* (1970) and *The Projector* (1971), both incorporate all the traditional surface elements that spell 'comics': panels, characters, balloons, brushwork, etc. Also clear is that Vaughn-James is refining his approach during this era. The progression from *Elephant* to *The Projector* is an obvious one, as is the progression from *The Projector* to *The Cage*. Only when you look at the jump from *Elephant* to *The Cage* do you see what a real artistic leap that is: *Elephant* is an interesting early experiment at an artsy comic book novel, and *The Cage* is a fully realized artistic masterpiece of the comics medium. To be fair, I should mention that there is another book, *The Park*, between *The Projector* and *The Cage*. In every way it is closer to *The Cage* than his previous books but it is a very short book (just a short story, really) and, in my opinion, is easily viewed as a warmup for his masterpiece.

Here I must stop and apologize. By this point in an introduction you would expect to have been given a summary of the book's plot. But I'm not even sure there is a plot to *The Cage*. I'm not confident I could list everything that happens in it, and I definitely couldn't put those events in order. I don't understand the book and I don't expect to understand the book at any point in the future. This is not because I haven't paid attention. In fact, I've paid *great* attention, giving the book extraordinary scrutiny. A few years ago I went through *The Cage* page by page, carefully noting and diagramming exactly what I thought was going on in each picture and its accompanying text. I tried to puzzle out how the words and images connected (or didn't connect), what symbols recurred throughout the book and what they might mean, how time operated within the story and, ultimately, what the story meant. It was hard going. I came away with a fair amount of insight, but in the end I remained perplexed. Which is what I suspect Vaughn-James wanted. The book isn't meant to be understood in the conventional way we expect a book to be understood. It is a puzzle, a Möbius loop, a labyrinth. At the centre of that labyrinth is a cage.

What is the cage? I don't think there's one correct answer, but it's interesting that the first images in the narrative place us *inside* the cage, and then we finish the book from the same perspective. The cage appears to be not just a box but a machine of some sort – a mysterious machine, to be sure. Other infernal machines come to mind: Marcel Duchamp's *Bride Stripped Bare by her Bachelors, Even*, or Kafka's terrible Penal Colony device. Or the odd machines of Langdon Jones's experimental science fiction of the early seventies. These all share qualities with Vaughn-James's cage – elusive, dreamlike, frightening. I don't know what is going on in *The Cage* but it feels like it is something terrible. The cage appears to be mirrored by two other images, a pyramid and a room. I think they might all be the same thing. They swap places with each other throughout the book. Are they stand-

ins for the same meaning? What is a cage, a room, a pyramid? A prison, a shelter, a tomb? Certainly that closed room at the centre of the pumping station is a metaphor for something. There are more questions in the book than answers.

What is happening with time in *The Cage*? I can't help you there either. Certainly there are several distinct time periods in the book. We can perceive that time is passing because of the obvious effects of entropy on the objects before us: they decay and vanish. But then they reappear, untarnished. Only to decay again. Is time moving forward? Or is it going in reverse? In certain sequences, time shifts dramatically within the drawings while the narrated voice-over rolls ahead uninterrupted. Often, the past, present and future appear to be occurring at the same moment (or at least in quick succession). Perhaps that whirling cylinder alluded to in the heart of the book (yet another machine? or, the cage again, in a further disguise?) is a kind of centrifuge, spinning out waves of distorted time? Or maybe time isn't moving at all. Is it solidified, frozen in place? Isn't all time halted in the beauty of the comic book panel?

There don't appear to be any characters in *The Cage*. In fact, there are no human figures at all. Still, one feels a human presence everywhere in the book. The detritus of human life is littered throughout the broken rooms and hallways of the pumping station. Sometimes the rooms and the objects are pristine, sometimes they're a terrible mess. Often the objects are machines themselves – cameras, tape recorders, microphones, binoculars – and they're all sensory devices. Sometimes these devices bind themselves together into scarecrow-like assemblages, which must be meant as human stand-ins –

it's hard not to interpret the endless images of bound rags as human bodies. Perhaps something of a holocaust occurred here. Is that why the cage is so menacingly composed of barbed wire?

What is a pumping station anyway? A facility that pumps substances from one place to another? What 'substance' is being pumped here? The only thing appearing to pass through the station is time. Can you 'pump' time? There are many startling images in the book depicting bizarre 'gushes' surging through the stations' corridors – gushes of ink or paper, leafy plants, garbage, even bound rags. Are they pumping through from one place to another? One time to another? Is the pumping station part of a system? Certainly, a pumping station as we know it, is connected to a network of other utilities. If I were to venture a guess, this pumping station is a focal point between the various times and realms seen in the book. A filter of some kind between these realms maybe? Between orderliness and decay? Maybe? It's all maybe.

And what is the cage? Why are we watching from within it? Is the viewer the prisoner in the cage? Locked inside the cage? Is it the cage of time? The cage of perception? Maybe the cage is reality itself?

I am not up to answering these questions. And neither was Vaughn-James. I doubt even he ever knew the answers.

But getting the answers isn't all that important to the experience of reading his book. *Experience* is the key word here. You experience *The Cage* rather than understand it.

I was gratified to see Martin Vaughn-James mention Resnais's *Last Year at Marienbad*

as an influence in his preface. I think that film might be an excellent model for how to best experience *The Cage*. It's a rich, dreamlike, hypnogogic film, ideally watched in a surrendered manner, allowing the film to simply flow over you rather than trying to force it into a narrative straightjacket. The film loops back upon itself, repeating and elaborating until a cumulative effect is achieved. It's my favourite film, and that surely helps explain why I keep coming back to *The Cage* even though it continues to perplex.

Even today, when a healthy number of serious, artistic – even masterful – graphic novels have been published, *The Cage* stands as a singular work. No one else has come up with anything quite like it. It's a truly unique book that I am proud was published in this country. Martin Vaughn-James wasn't a Canadian, nor did he stick around here all that long, but it's a Canadian book to me; I'm convinced its tone fits snugly alongside the works of Marshall McLuhan, Glenn Gould and Norman McLaren. I am grateful to have it as part of my artistic heritage.

It's a challenging book, but I hope a new generation of readers will come to appreciate his masterwork. My fondest hope is that young Canadian cartoonists will embrace the ambition that Martin Vaughn-James showed as a narrative artist. If it were up to me, he'd be regarded as a national treasure.

Preface

The Cage: *Image-making machine*

Martin Vaughn-James

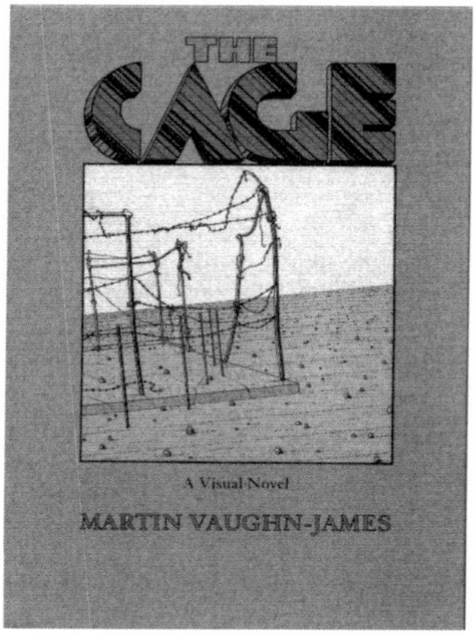
THE CAGE
A Visual Novel
MARTIN VAUGHN-JAMES

A book with no story, a book with no characters. A comic book that doesn't look much like a comic. A strange idea? Where did it come from? Out of the blue?

In the summer of 1968 I arrived in Toronto from London with my wife, Sarah, and a folder of crudely drawn surrealistic comic strips. The counterculture was in full swing: these were the Trudeau years – draft dodgers, Vietnam, the FLQ, the Canadian Identity – Paris '68, U.S. assassinations, Watergate, Pop Art, Bacon, Dylan and Zappa, Borges, Bergman and Beckett, Godard and Pasolini ... and all the rest. Psychedelic graphics were rampant, the fog of distant revolutions drifted through the safe, tree-lined streets of Canada.

My little comic strips and illustrations were published primarily in *Saturday Night* magazine and the *Toronto Star*, as well as in various underground journals of the period; I remember a two-page comic about pollution. From Montreal I sent our friend Richard an entire letter in the form of a comic book. If two pages, why not ten? If ten, why not fifty?

Back in Toronto, in a room filled with suitcases and library books, Sarah read Céline while I drew my first album, *Elephant*. I didn't come from a culture of comics; my childhood was filled with my father's copies of *The Boy's Own Paper* and other illustrated relics of the Empire. My *Tintin* was the dearly beloved *Rupert Bear* (no speech balloons, separate images and texts) and *The Eagle*, a wholesome paper for English teenagers. On the other hand, my adolescence in Australia was marked by the incomparable *Mad* magazine of the late fifties with its marvellously anarchic satires and astonishing draftsmanship.

Elephant, my hastily but enthusiastically drawn surrealistic social satire, came out in 1970. The publishers gave it a subtitle to speed it on its way; they called it a 'boovie.' Among its many curiosities are images of a bottle of ink spilling over blank pages, the ink from which, of course, the drawings would be made. It would reappear as a mechanical metaphor in my next book, *The Projector*, published in 1971 by Stan Bevington of the now-legendary Coach House Press, home of all that was energetically new, however extreme, obscure, marginal or 'Canadada,' as we saw it. The Canada Council for the Arts at the time had a fierce policy of 'Canadian Identity' (as opposed to the overwhelming identity of the great giant below the 49th parallel); consequently, works of quality and originality were actively encouraged without demanding that beavers and lumberjacks make their symbolic appearance.

Around that time, a student friend, Janet, lent us a translated copy of Robbe-Grillet's *For a New Novel* and we subsequently read everything we could find: Simon, Pinget, Butor, etc.

In *The Projector* there are many drawings that prefigure *The Cage* – derilect rooms, objects falling through space, sequences of two or three pages with no characters at all, double-page spreads with deserts and urban landscapes. The idea that either we, the reader, are seeing things through the eyes of the central character, or that we have in some way replaced the character, is evident in the first two pages of the book. In fact, the house we see at the beginning and end is situated in reality a few Toronto streets away from the pumping station in the *The Cage*. To get from one to the other you must go through a park, the title and setting of my next little book, *The Park*.

If *The Projector* was done in parallel to the *nouveau roman*, *The Park* was in some ways both a homage to Butor and Robbe-Grillet, and a dry run for *The Cage*, which in fact I had already started when Coach House proposed a book of thirty-two pages.

American film noir, with its labyrinthine plots and heavily contrasted black and white photography, flashbacks and voice-over narrations, has always fascinated me, as well as rare so-called 'subjective' camera techniques, most notably in the first sequence of *Dark Passage*. Ray Milland directed and starred in a film noir with sound but no dialogue. Later, Godard would show us one character who didn't speak, with the voice of another we couldn't see. I could cite dozens of examples from the cinema of the sixties and early seventies, both European and American, that undoubtedly helped shape my thinking about the 'visual novel' around 1971–1972, but I'm fairly sure that *L'année dernière à Marienbad* had the greatest overt influence on *The Cage*.

In 1972, I won a project and travel grant from the Canada Council and went to Paris. There, in another small room on the Rue Saint-Séverin, I completed all the drawings for *The Cage* and met several people associated with Les Éditions de Minuit. The first issue of the literary review *Minuit* had just been published and I become a regular contributor with many *Cage*-like sequences.

Mallarmé had said something about creating a work of art out of nothing. As all artists and writers know, that 'nothing' is normally the dreaded blank page. If you are a graphic artist and are doing a book, that blank page becomes a diptych, a double-page spread, and every time you turn the page (in *Elephant* I actually incorporated the hand turning the page into the titles of the book) you are confronted with another diptych that replaces the preceding one and anticipates the next – an obvious fact, but an absolutely fundamental principal for a narrative 'created out of nothing' such as *The Cage*.

But the memory doesn't work neatly like flashbacks in a movie. Time is elastic and non-chronological, cyclical for the Gods and unidirectional for us mortals. We know also that the eye sees only what the brain allows it to see and ignores the rest, that our emotions change with time and consequently alter what we live as well as what we have lived. And so some simple, straightforward narrative was out of the question. Blank pages demand to be filled, especially by someone who suffers from chronic *horreur du vide*. To fill them I needed some kind of generator that could produce atemporal, self-accumulating images that would roll like snowballs and rise like houses of cards. I borrowed the facade of an electric pumping station for my 'image generator' (I suppose I liked its neo-classical style), and invented a sort of infernal spinning piano-roll to produce my 'voice-over' text.

In effect, this machine already existed; my *Projector* was a sort of image-producing train on rails, rusty but ready for one last trip. Perhaps *The Cage* is its final spectacular presentation, its last slide show on earth. Fuelled by the basically simple idea of murdering the 'character' and of recreating or disposing of the evidence, the engine is cranked up and set in motion. It plunges forward and backward through space and time, consuming its own tail (or tale), spitting out pages and pictures in ever more complex combi-

nations as it glides or lurches down labyrinths of its own making, lending us all its optical and perceptual paraphernalia in the hope that we might see differently, as if through a pair of four- dimensional spectacles.

But see what, exactly? Thirty years later I have no satisfactory answer, an author orphaned by his own creation, baffled and pleasantly surprised to see that the monster has once again arisen, like our old friend Nosferatu, from its unquiet slumber.

Martin Vaughn-James
Brussels, February 2006.

THE CAGE

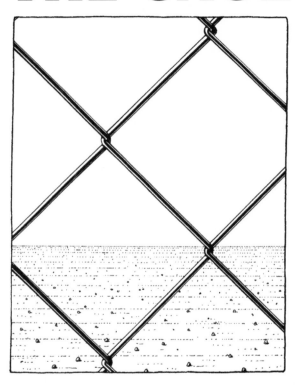

for Sarah
*through the arcades, indestructible longing casts its dangerous
and lovely shadow on the heart*

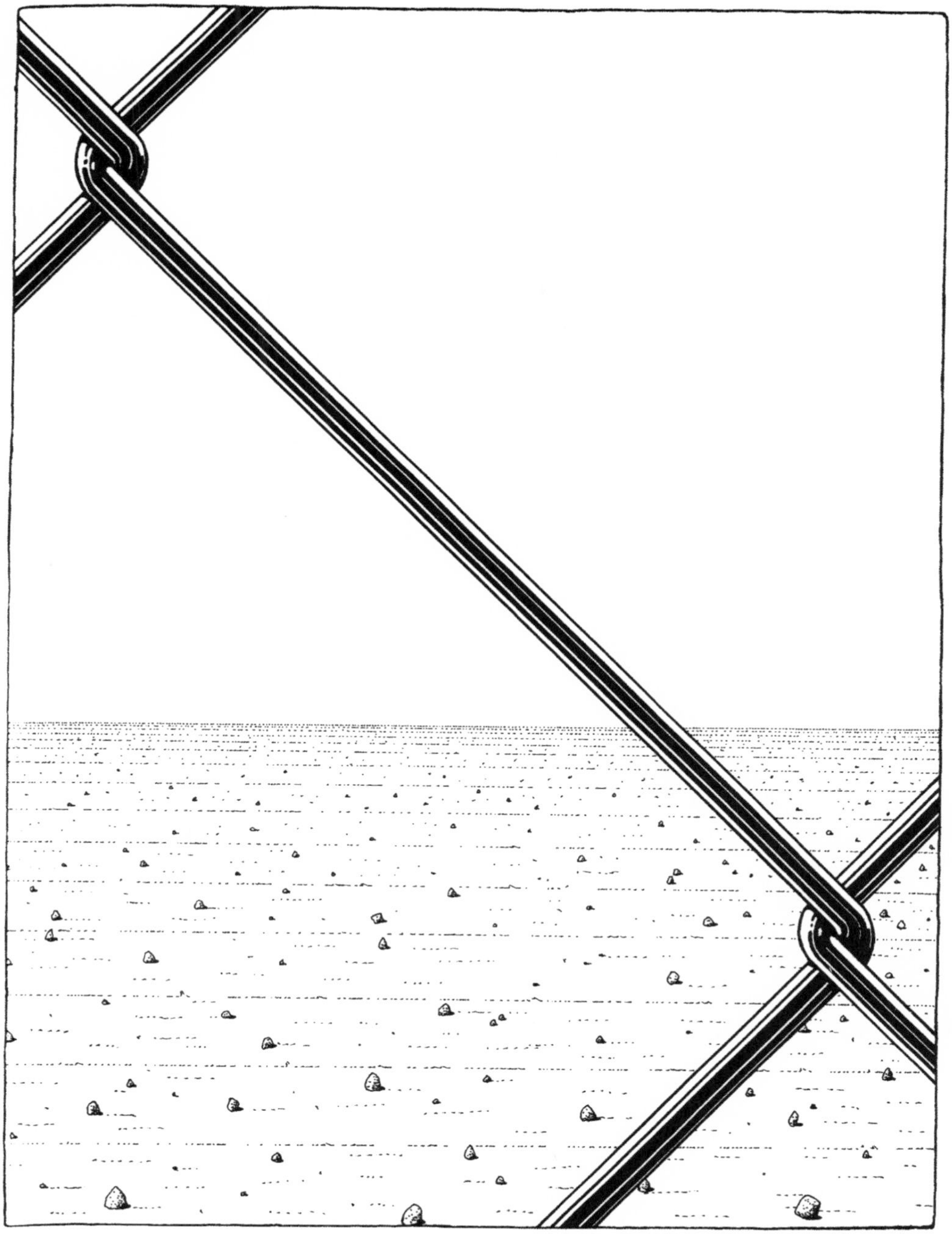

... the cage stands as before ... unfinished and already decayed

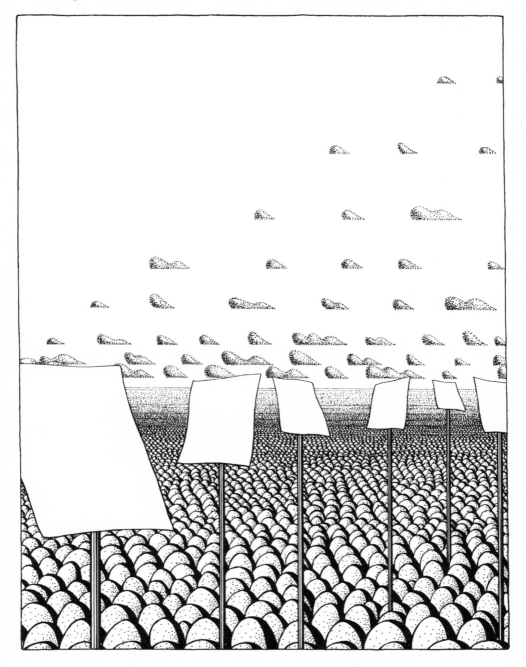

as if its construction had been abruptly and inexplicably arrested ...

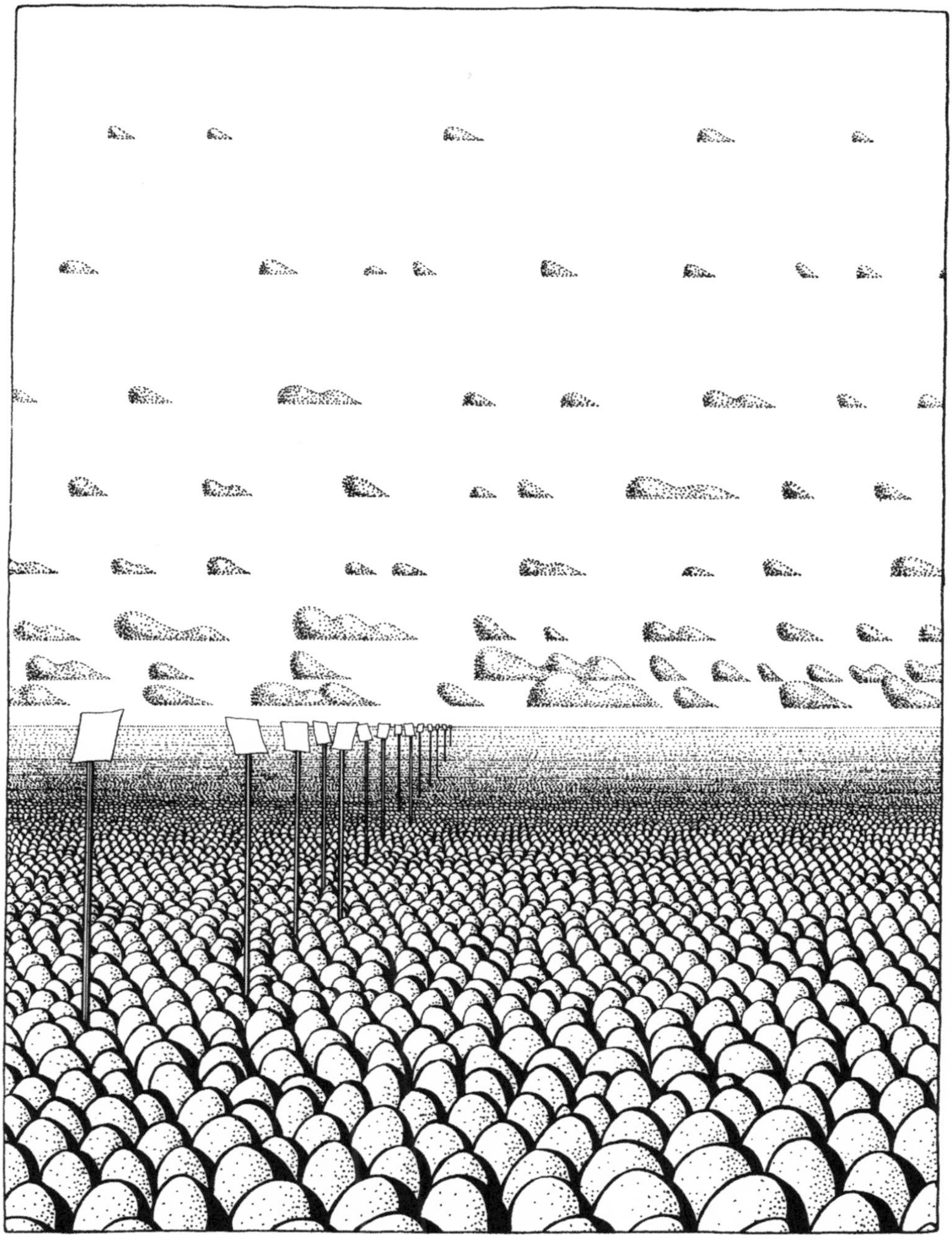

... its builders overtaken in their endeavour by some event

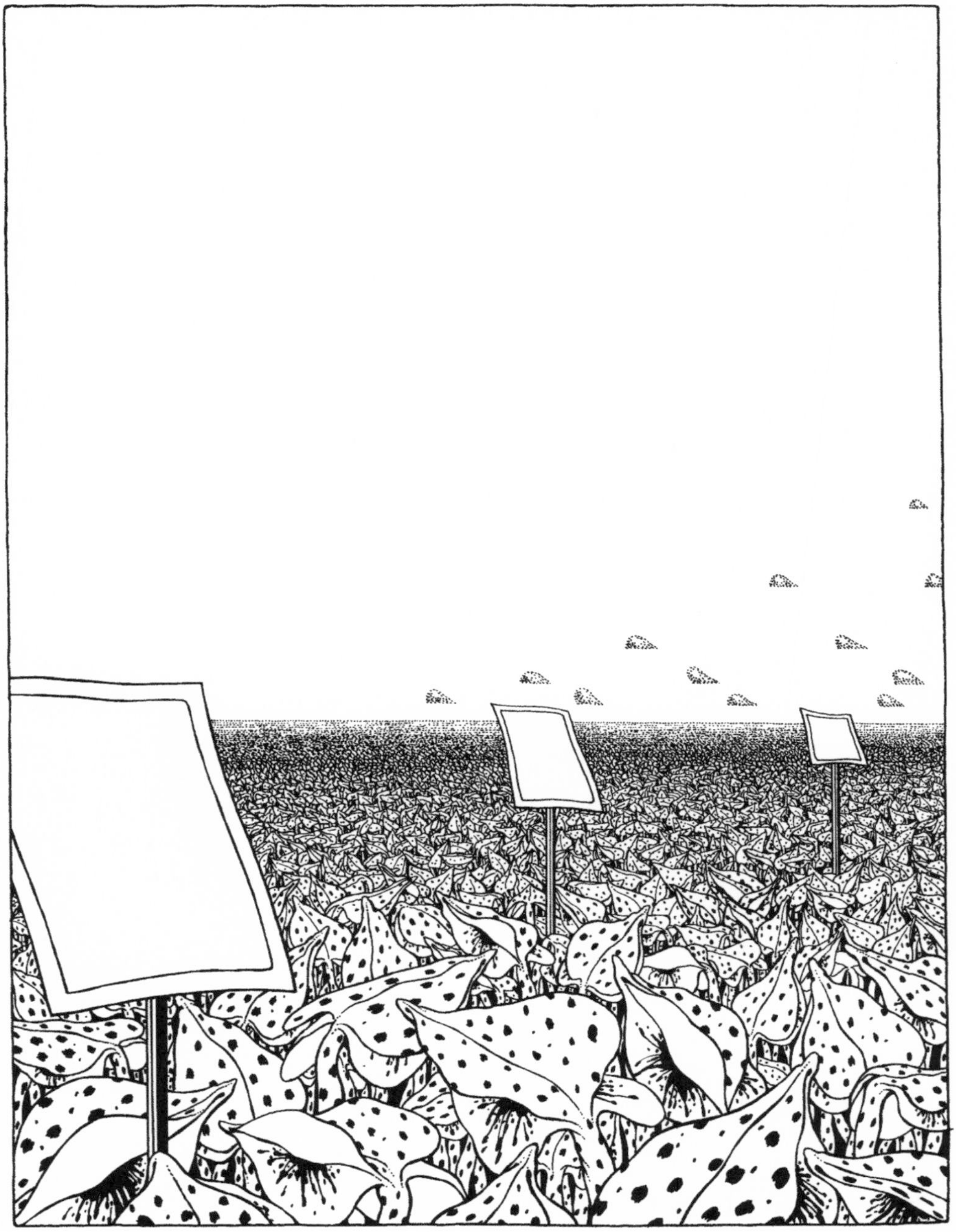

which for all their skill they had never for an instant anticipated

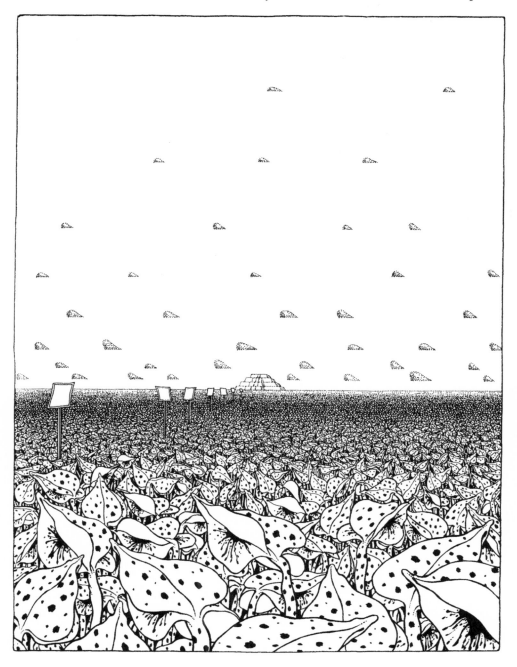

... an eruption so sudden and so violent that it reduced to rubble

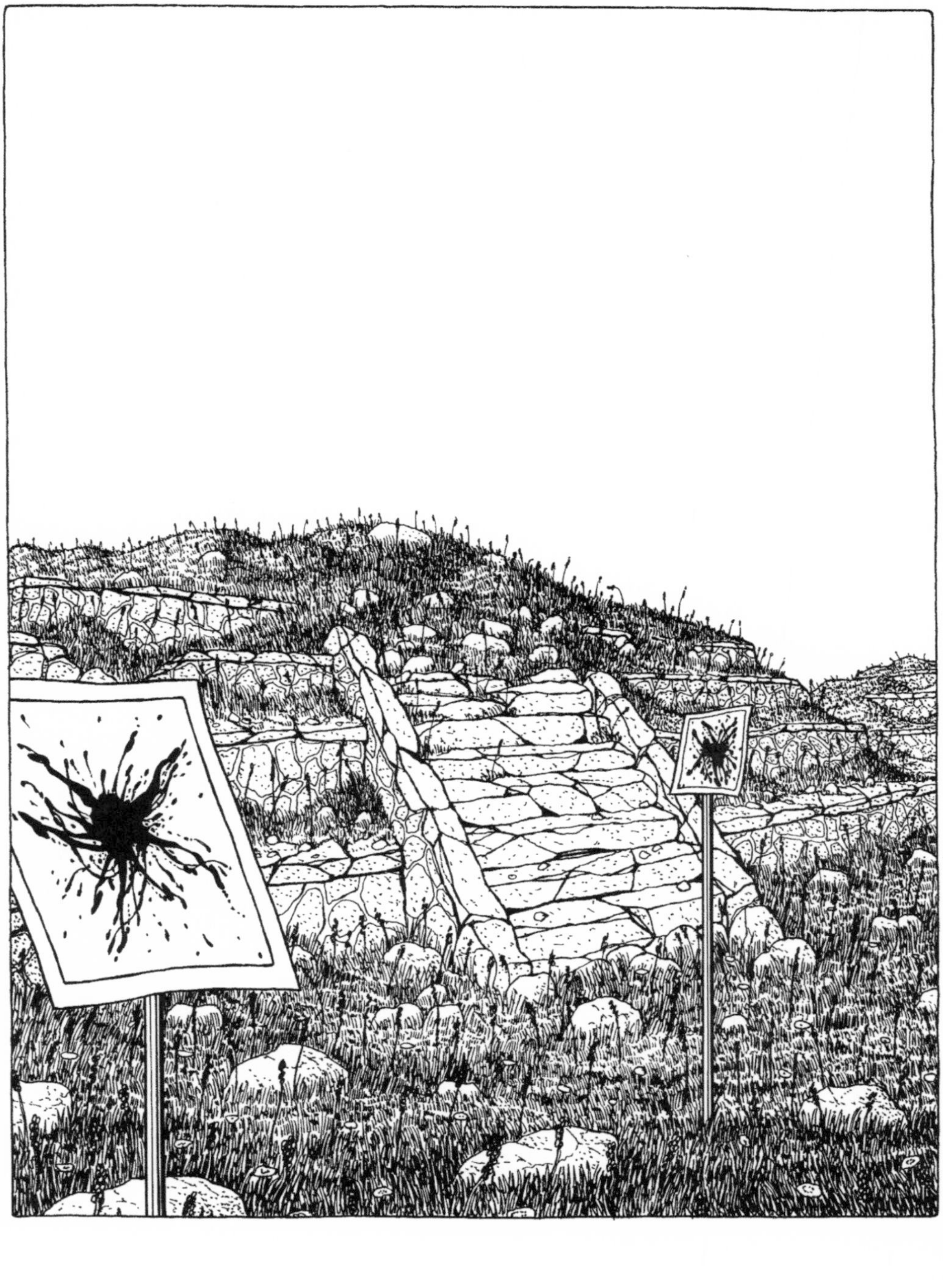

the elaborate structure (of which the cage was merely one feature)

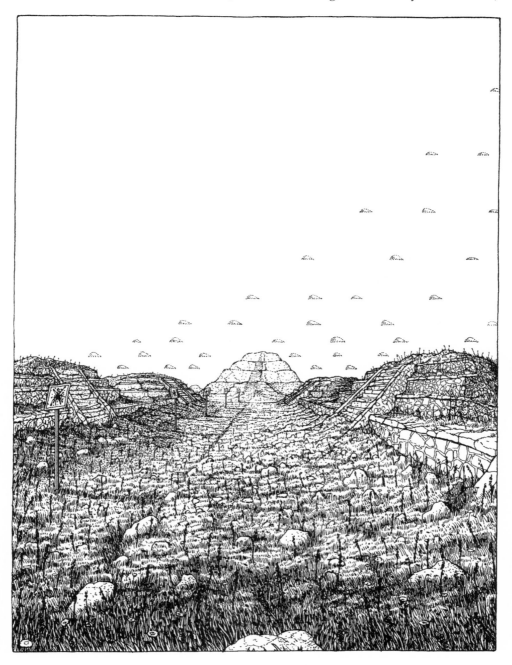

one facet of a complex network of forms arranged according to some logic

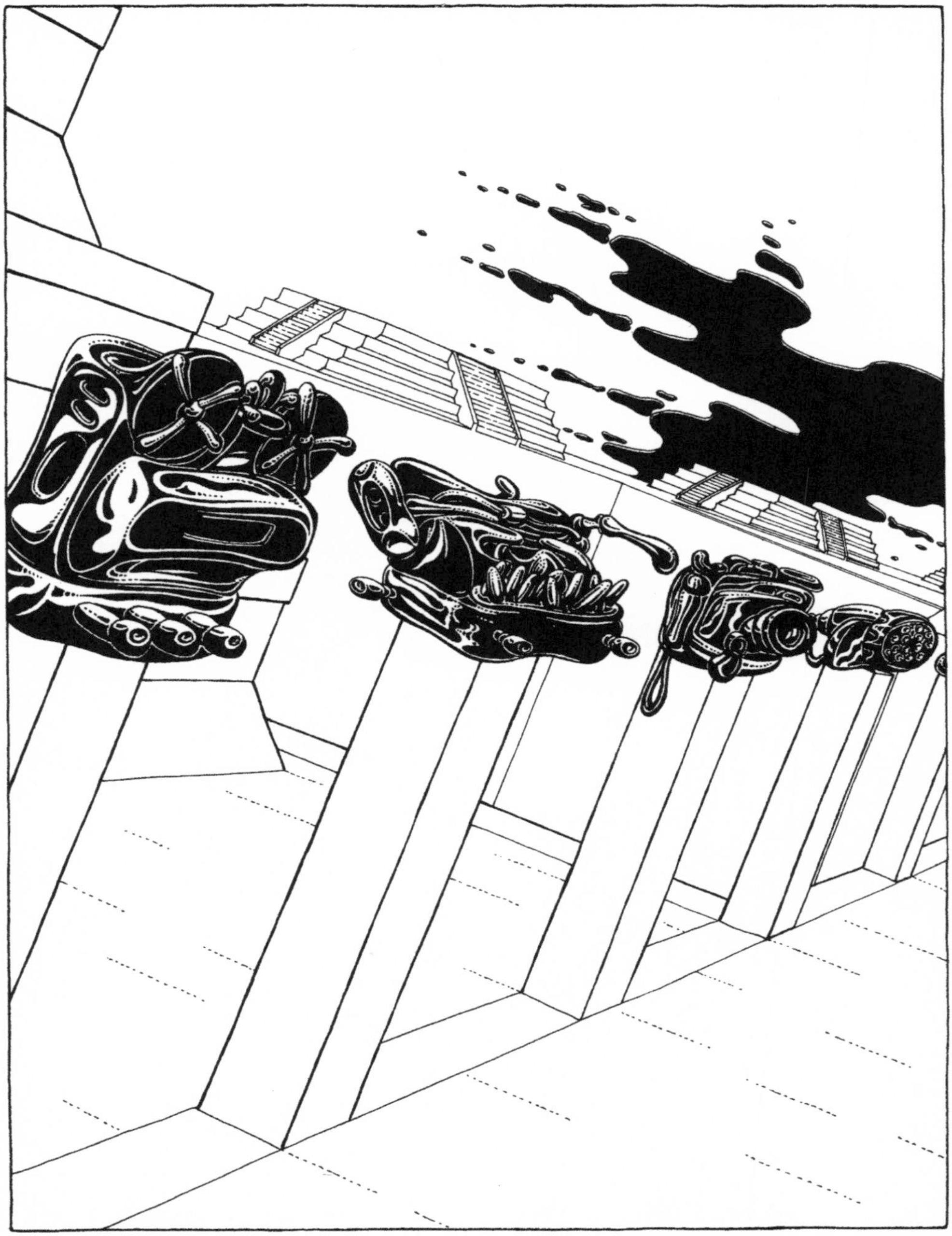

separate and alien to the surrounding desolation ...

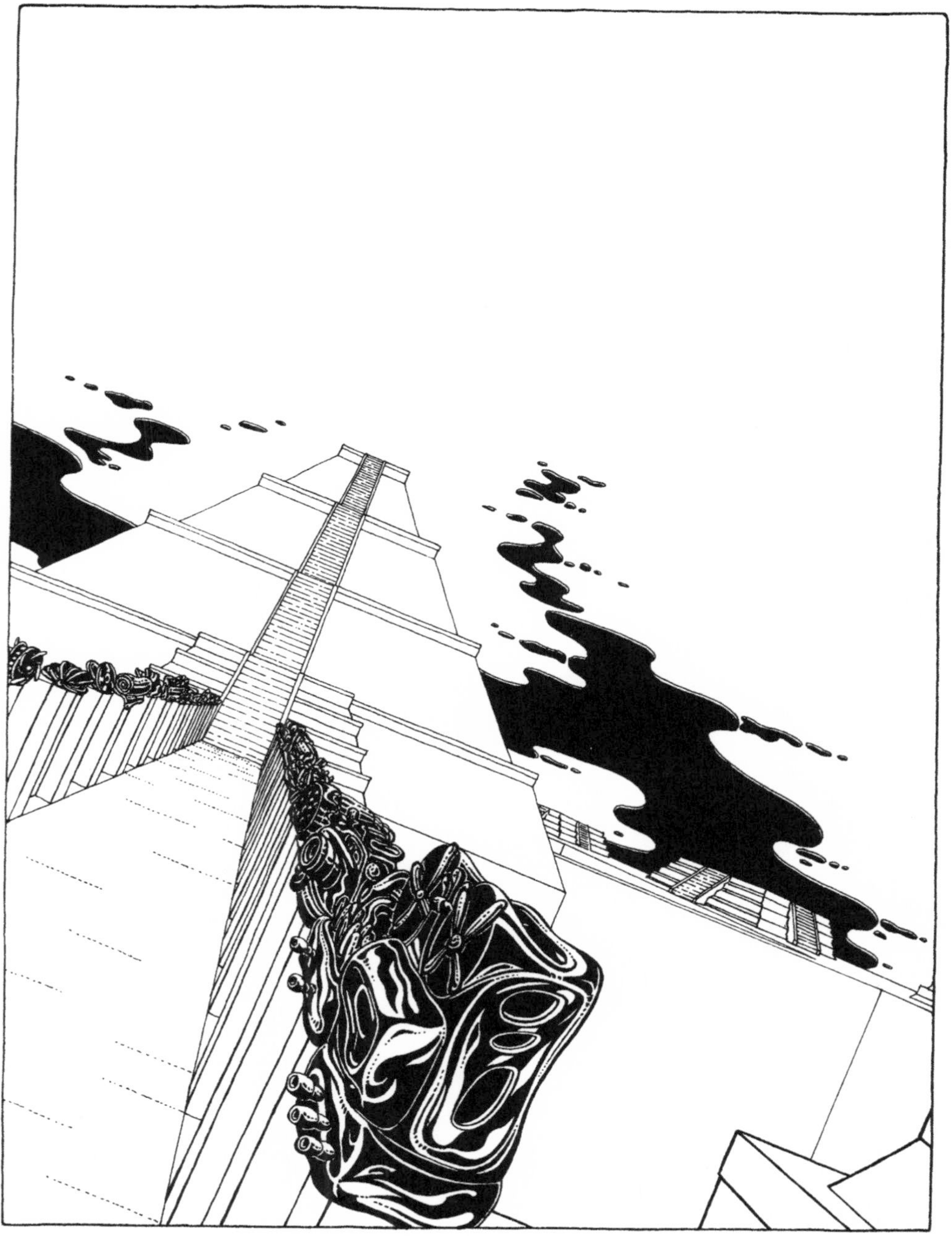

a labyrinth of distorted signs stretching out across the plain ...

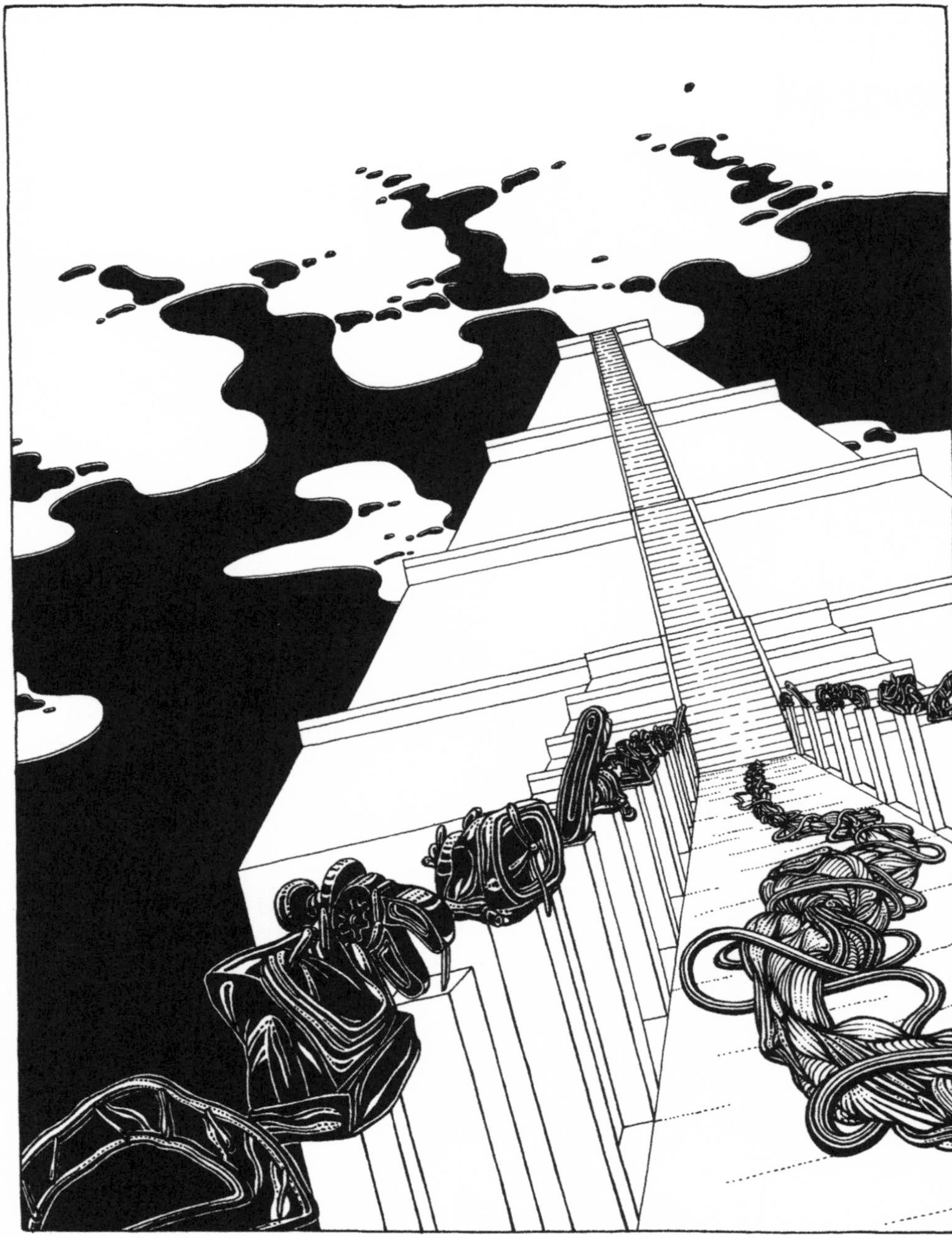

a wild attempt to contain the inevitable flood of mute destruction

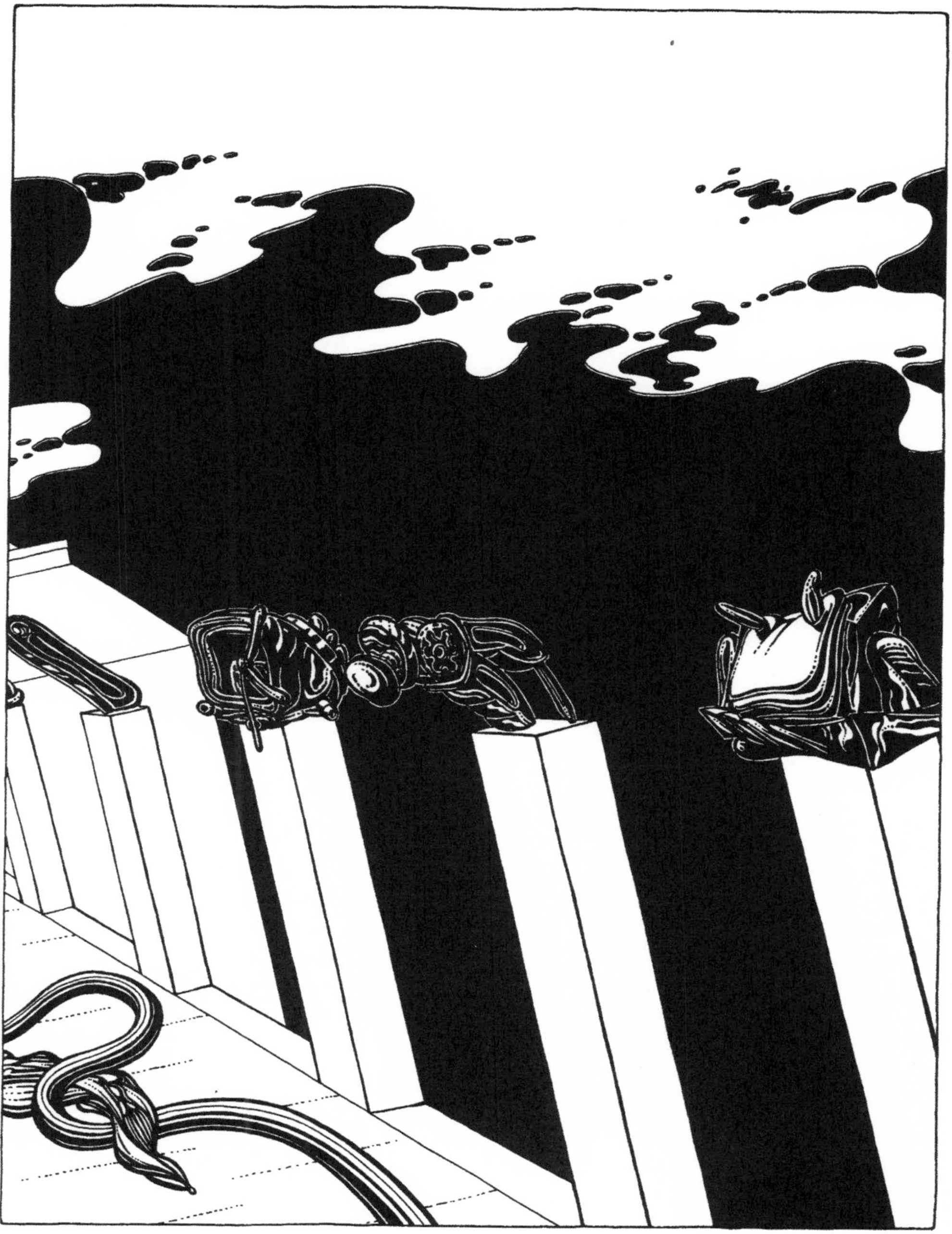

... a string of bloodied rags and broken nails obliterating everything

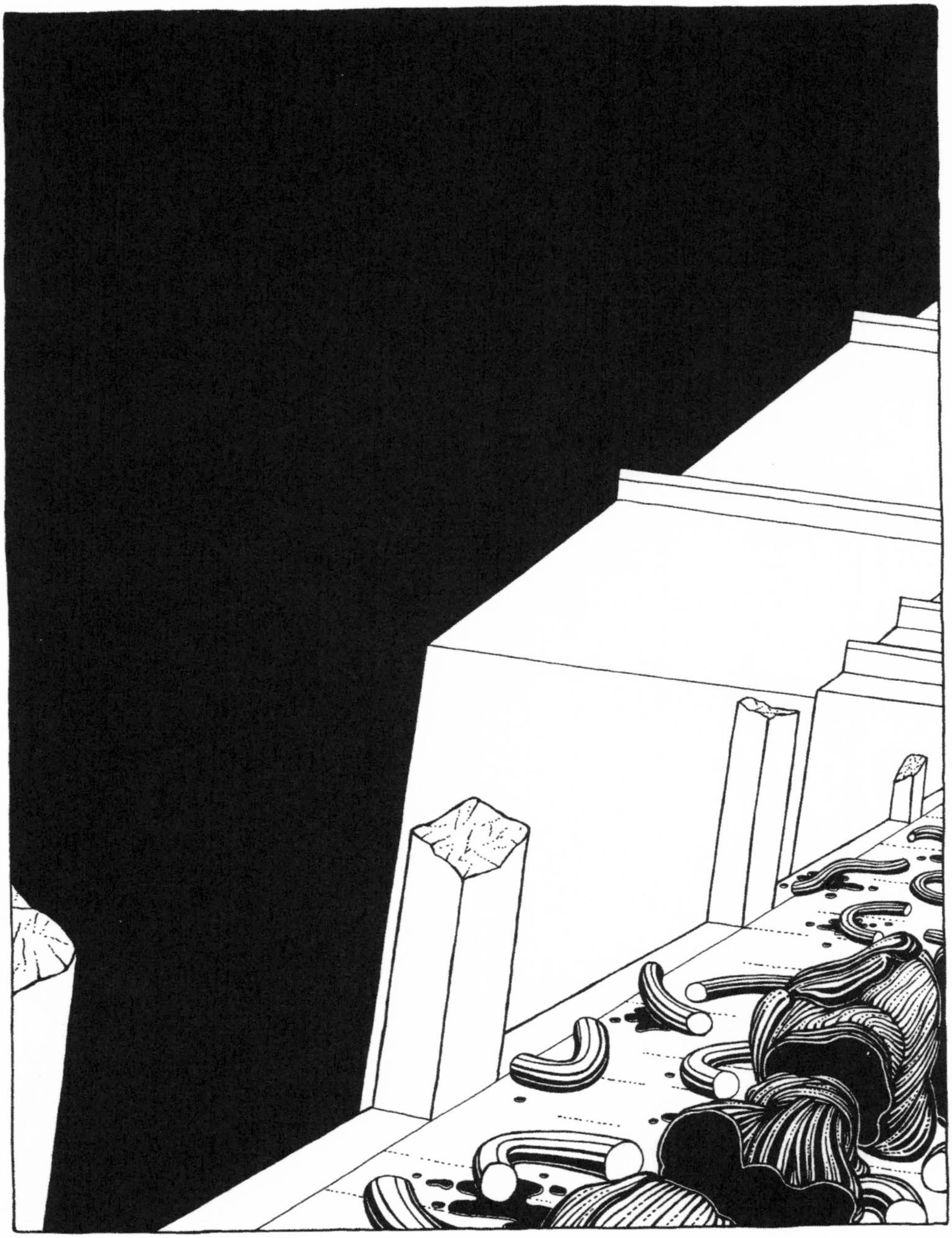

... but this barren cube ... significant only because it remains ...

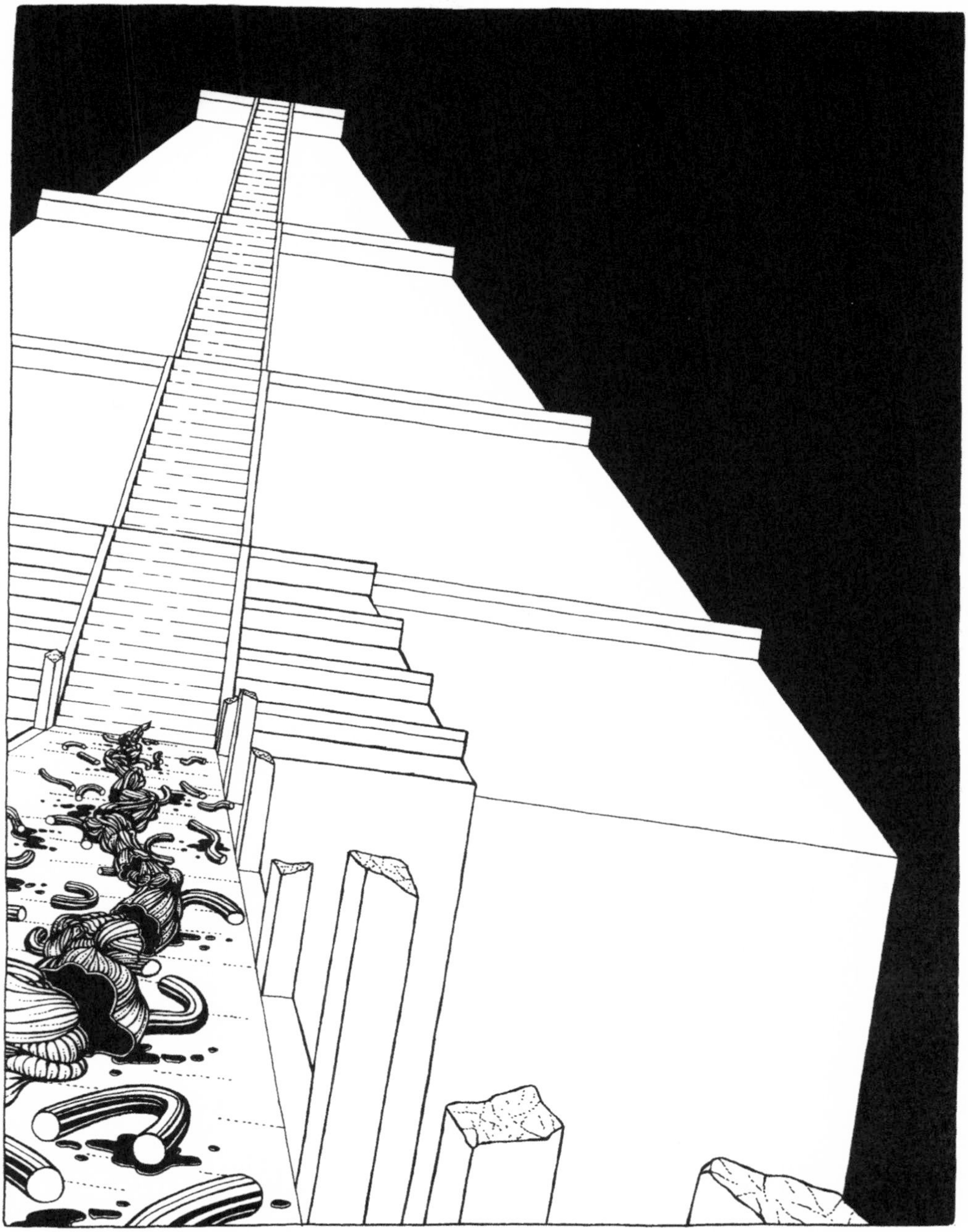

an empty analogy ... a vacuous, stale and airless bag of words ...

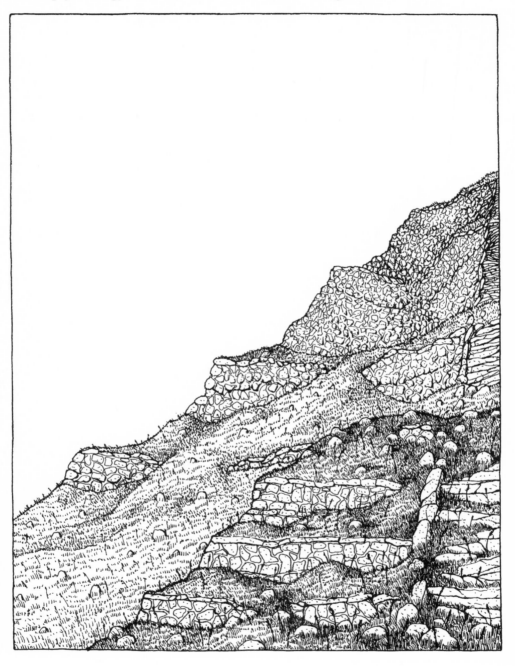

snatched from countless possibilities to give shape and substance

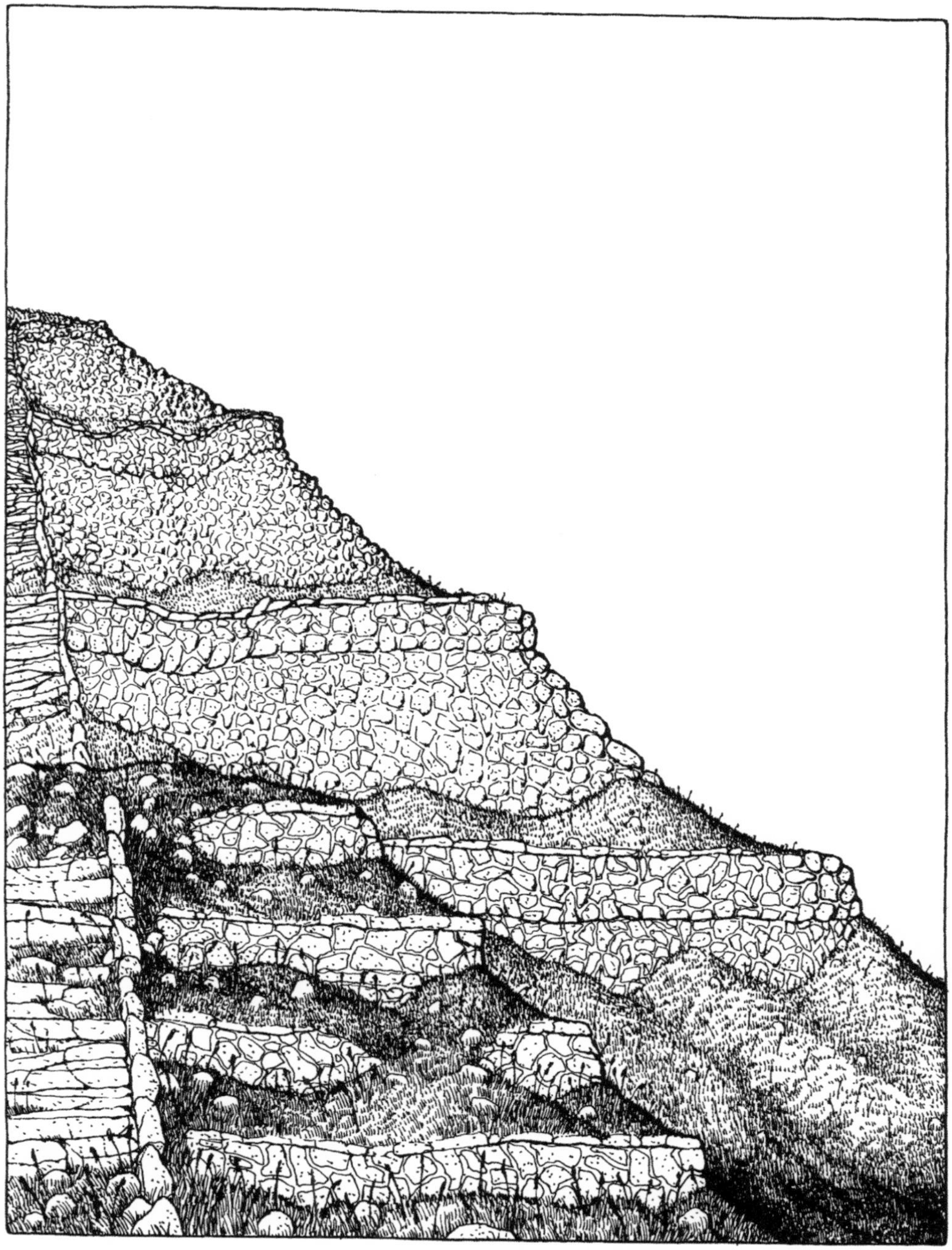

... scattered fragments serving only as a point of reference

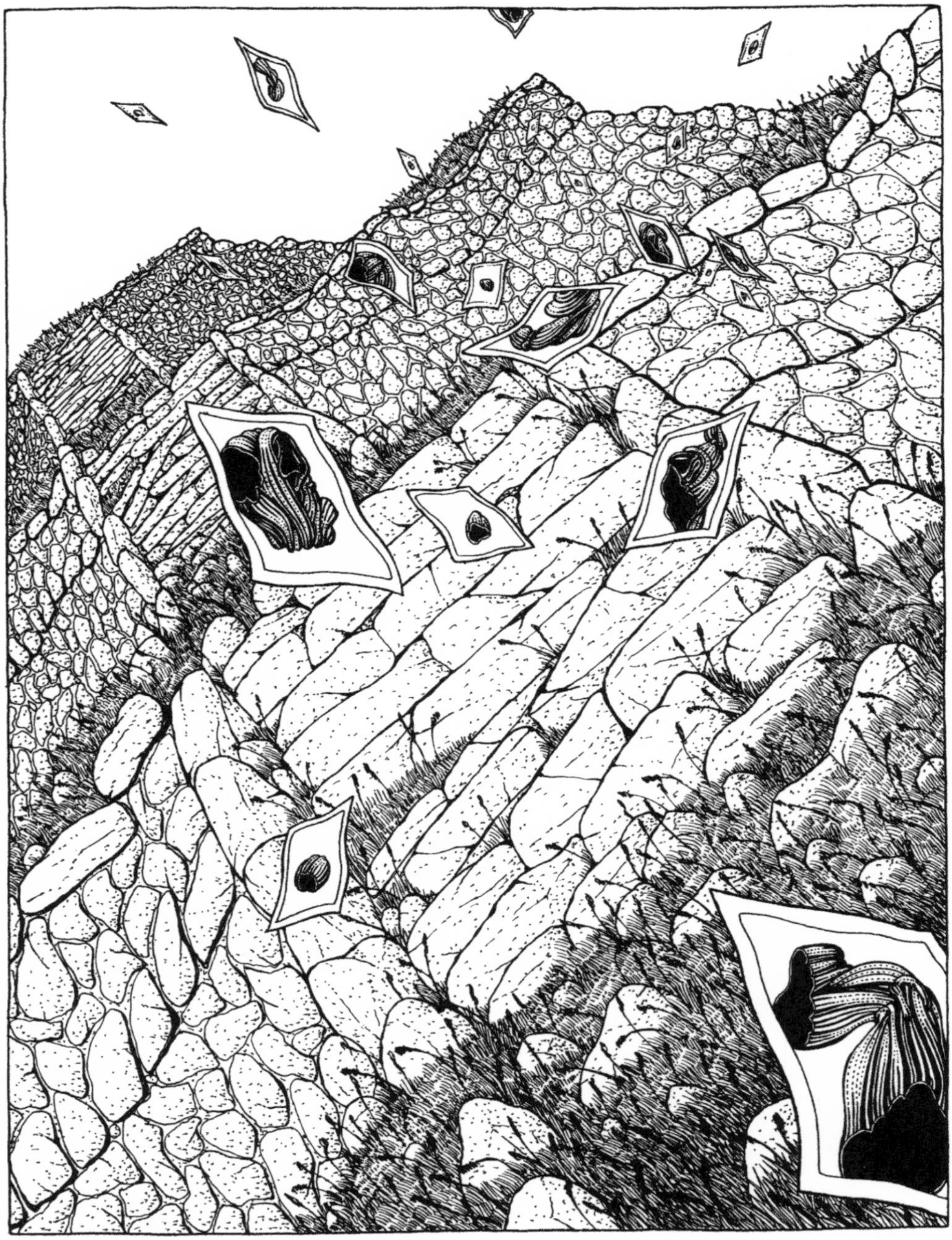

in this attempt to locate those elements which remain constant

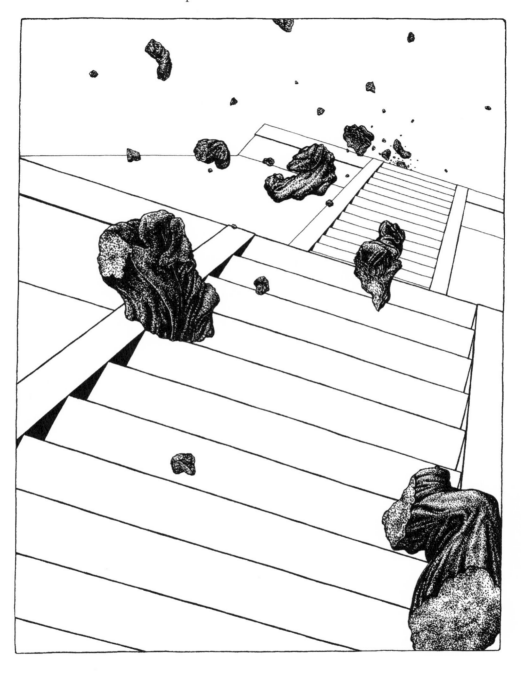

... those particles immune to chaos and decay ...

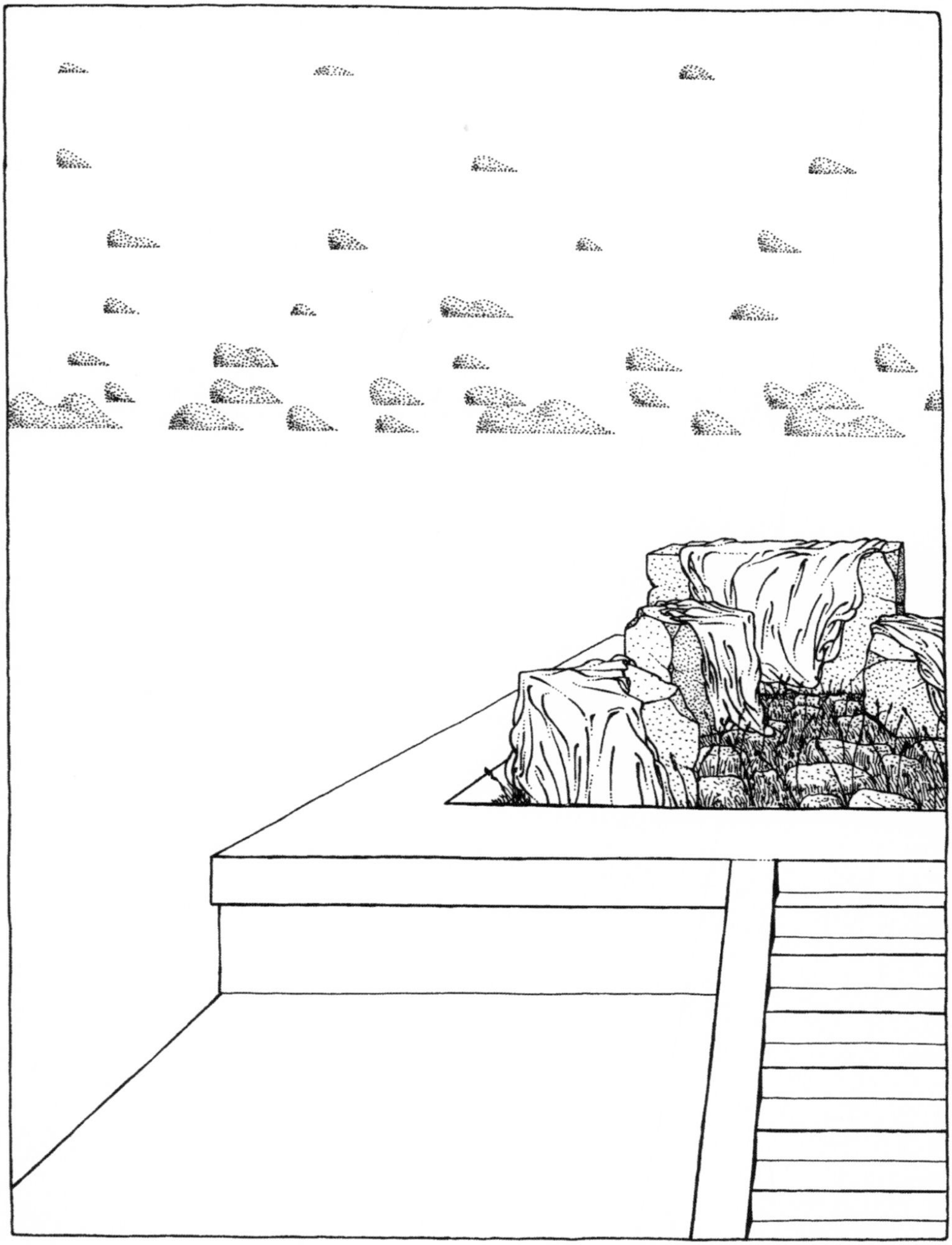

that shape which has been set down with such belief in its permanence

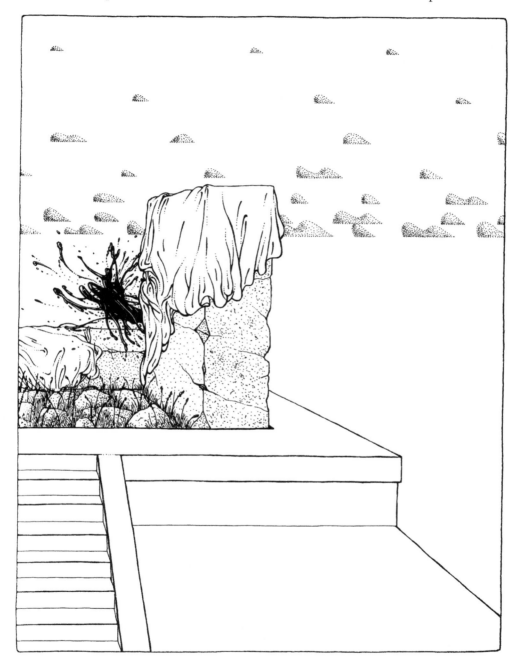

but in here ... after all ... what?

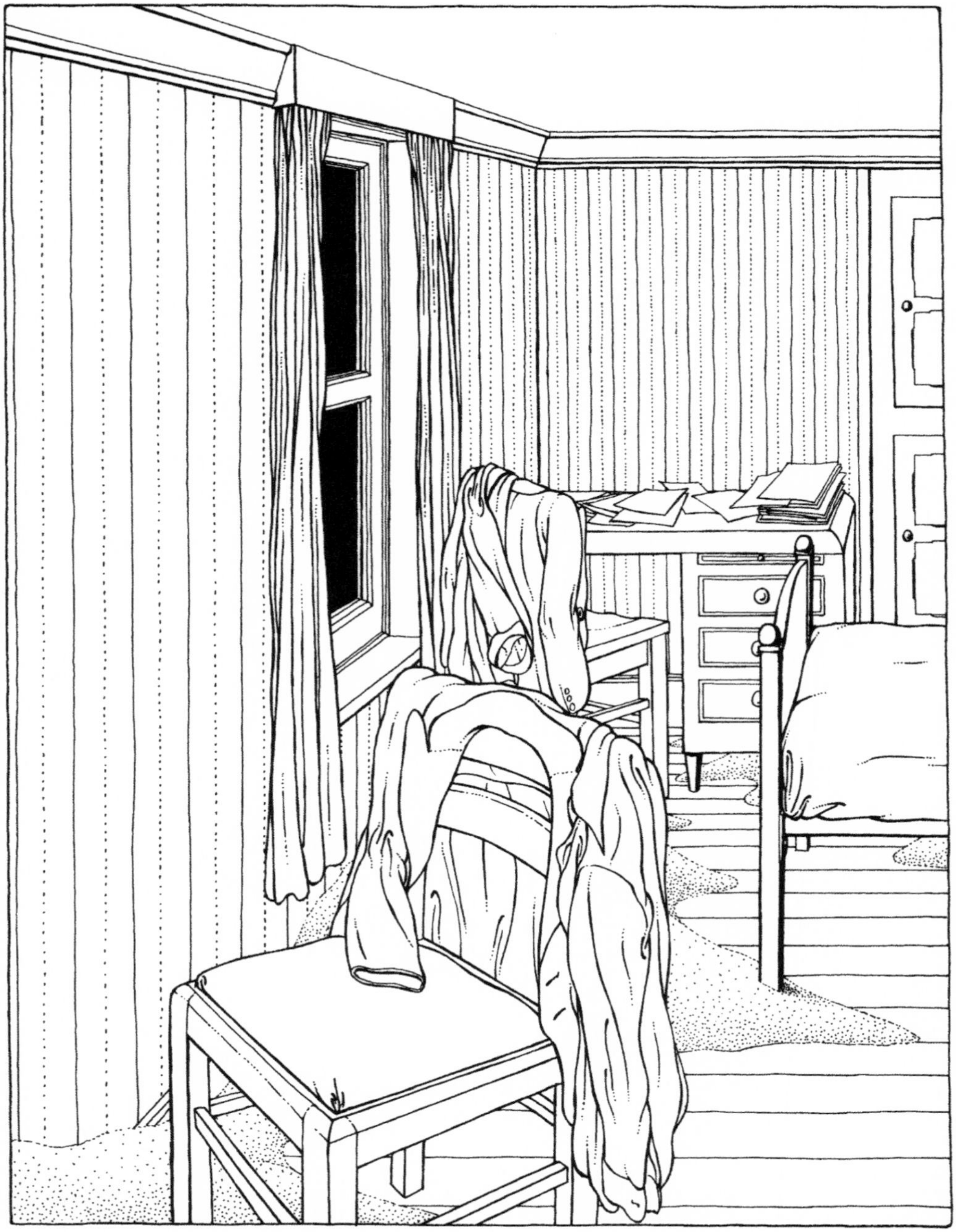

... a modest cubicle ...

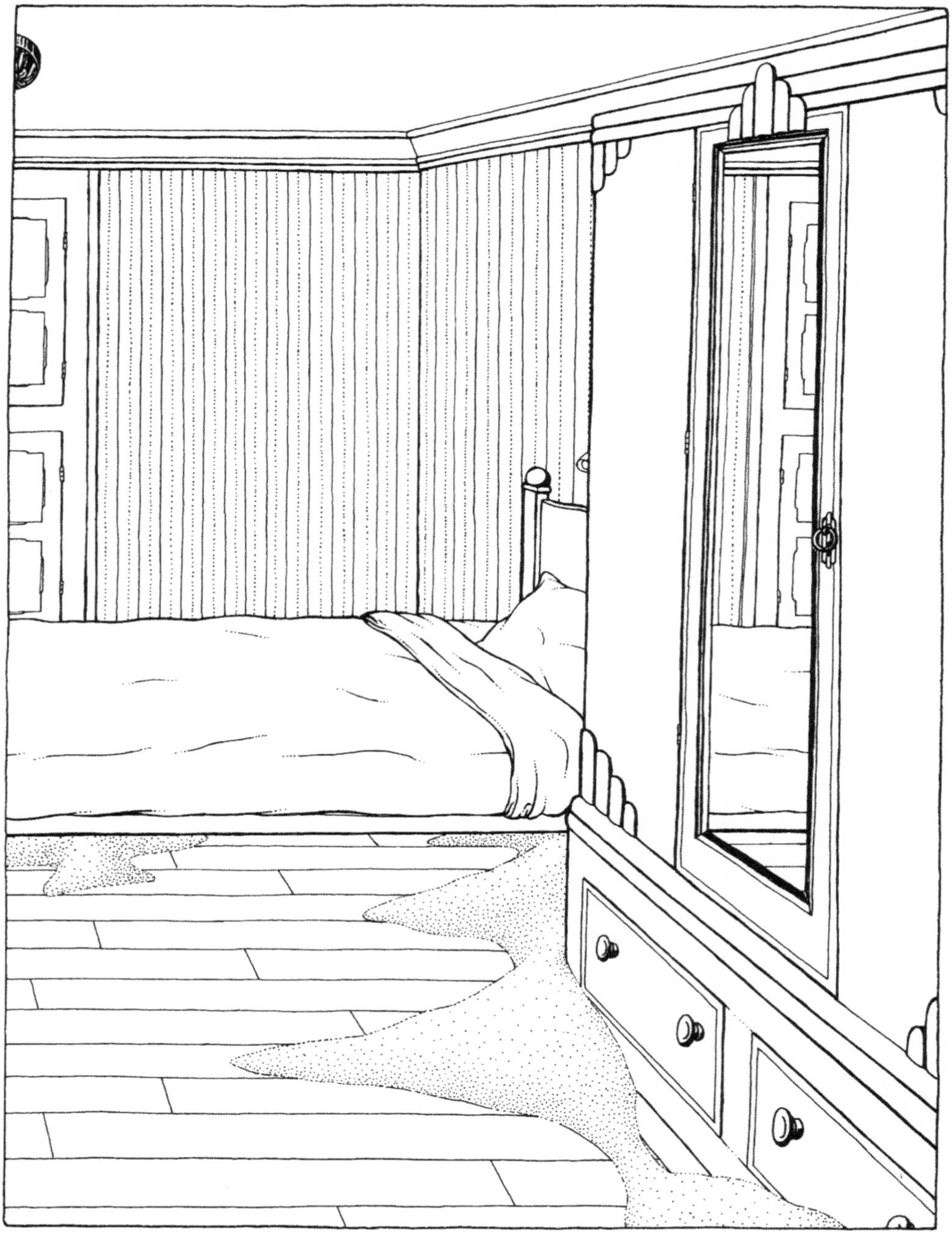

... a few familiar forms stagnating in utility ...

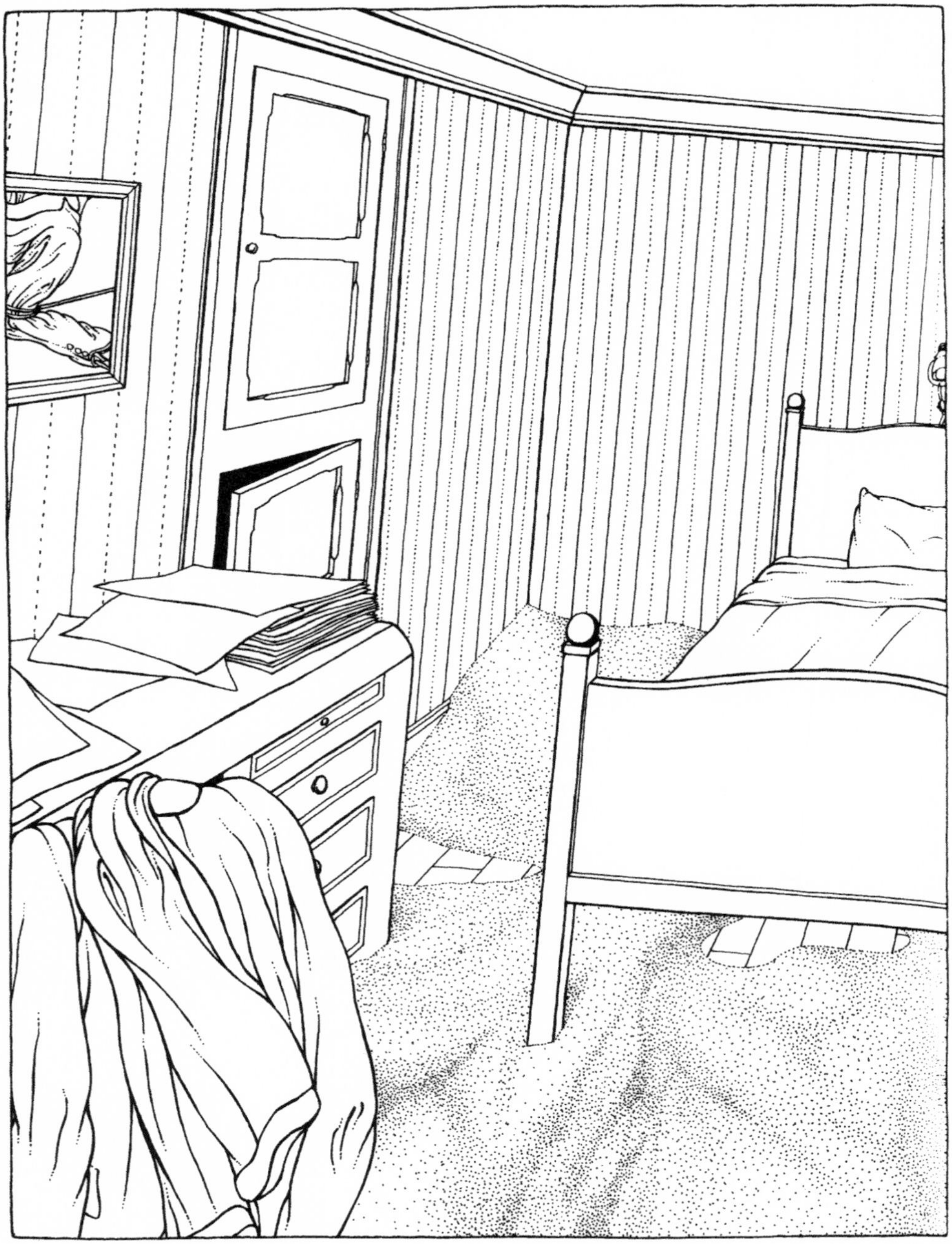

... remote ... banal ...

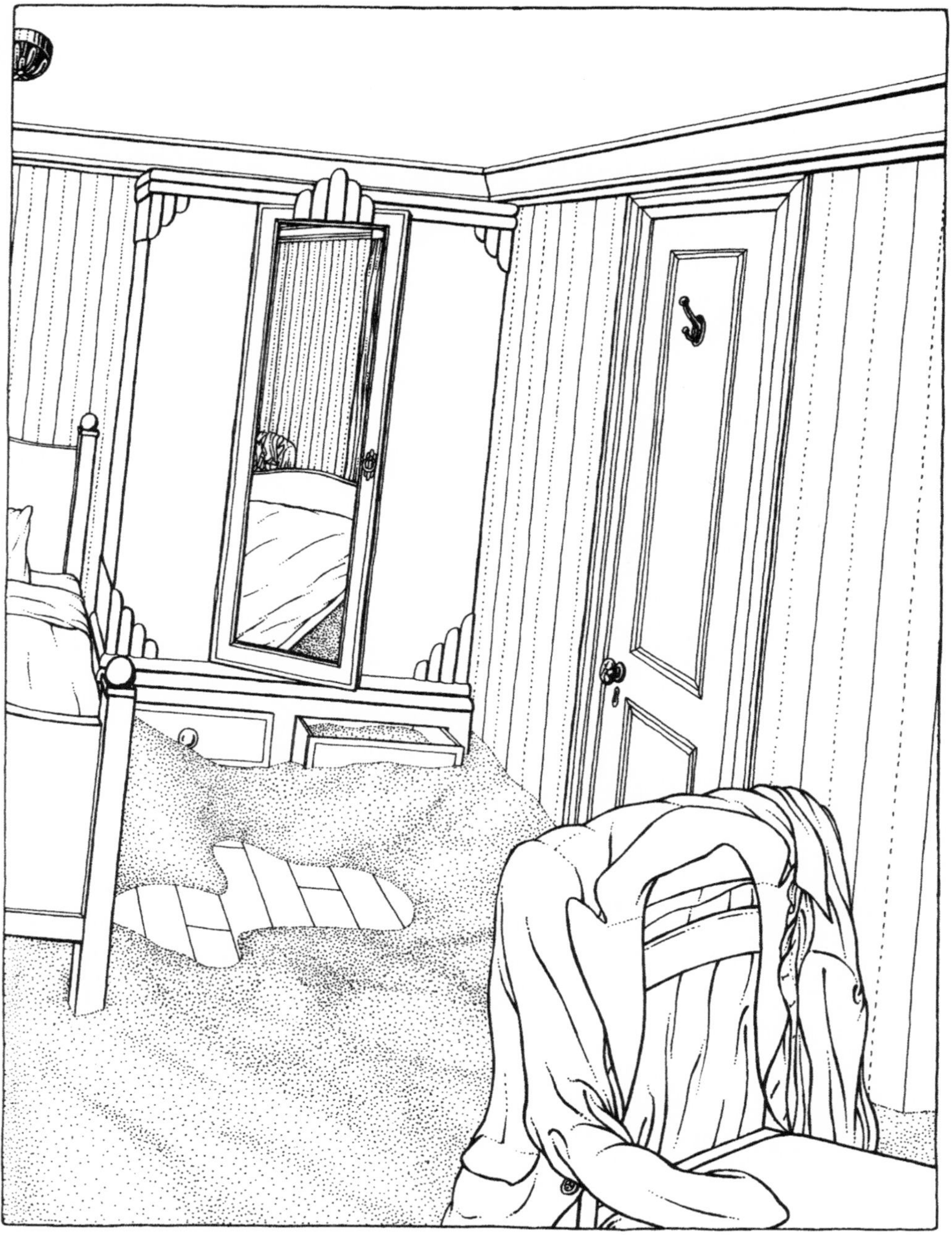

... concealing nothing ...

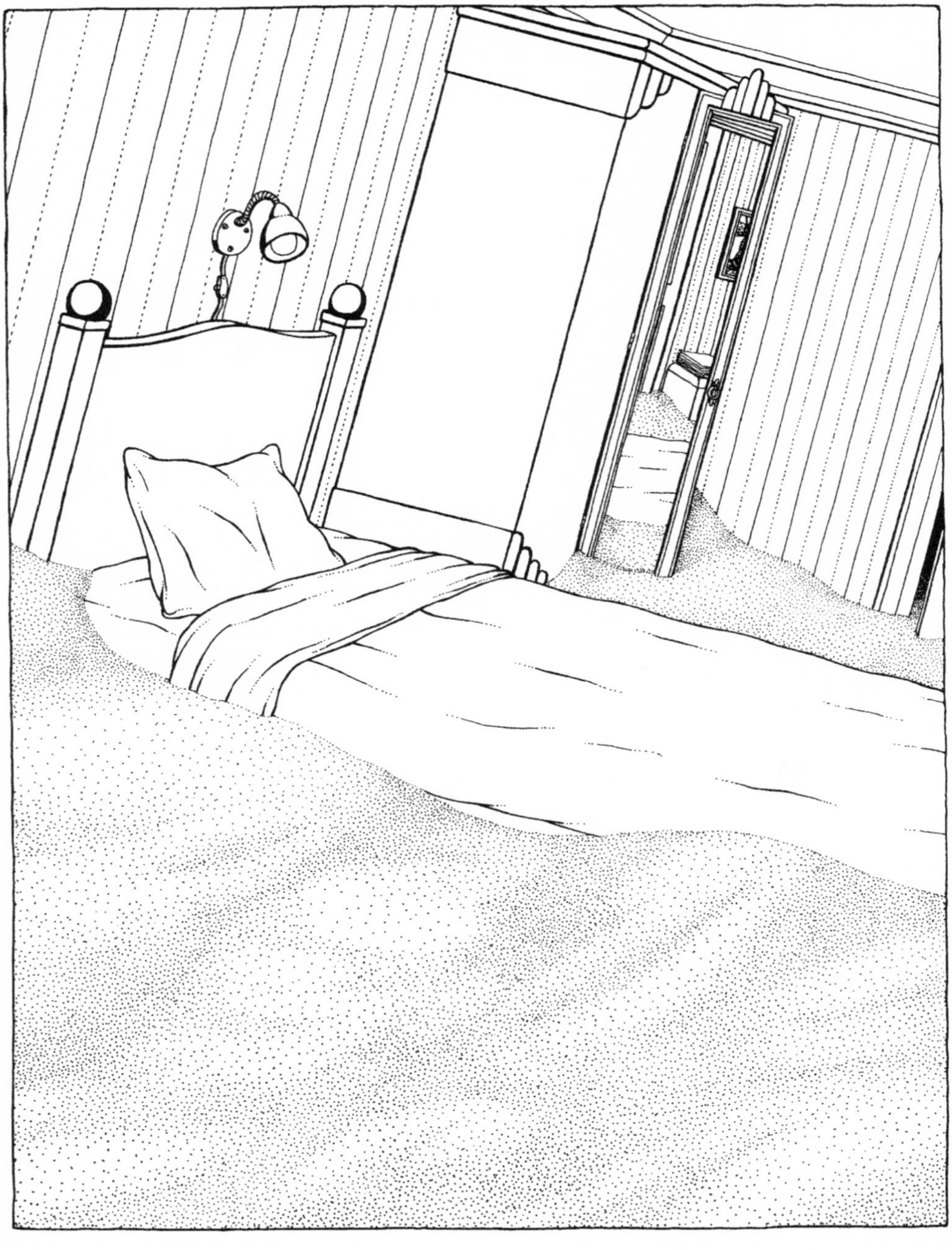

... beneath their single and continuous surface ...

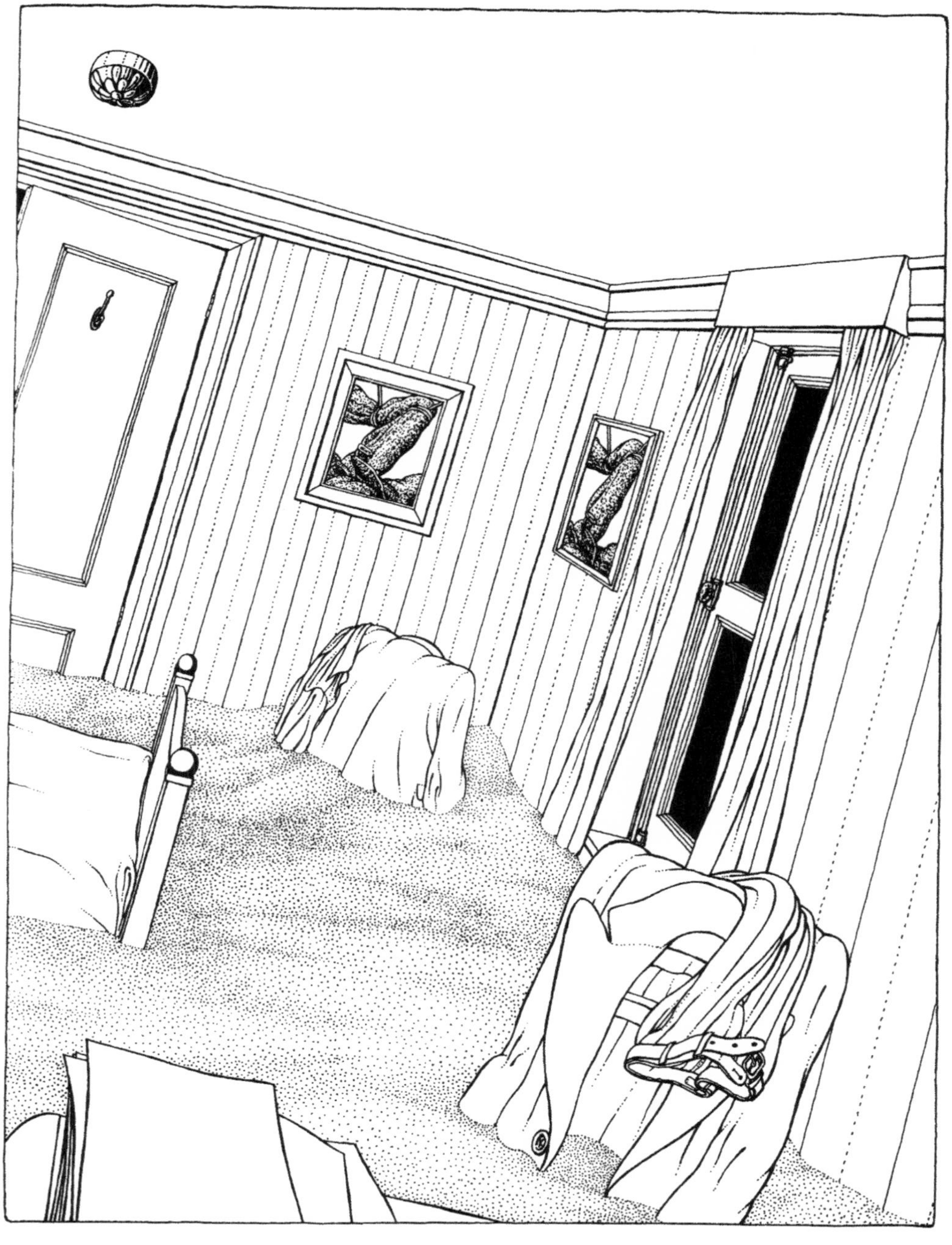

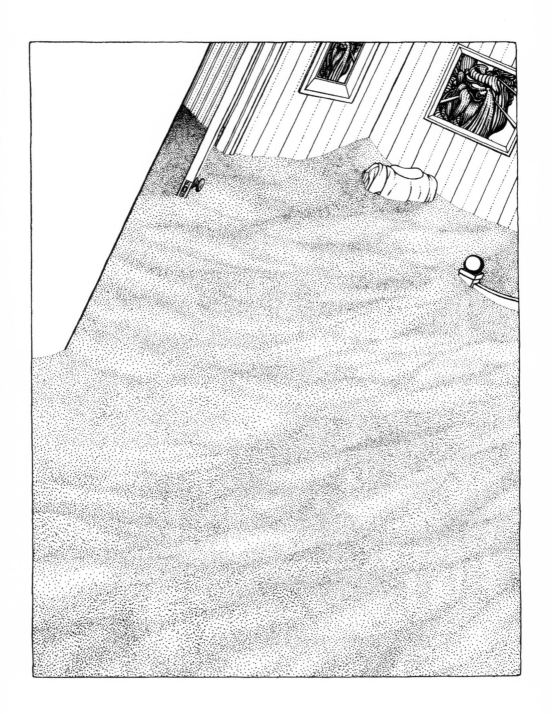

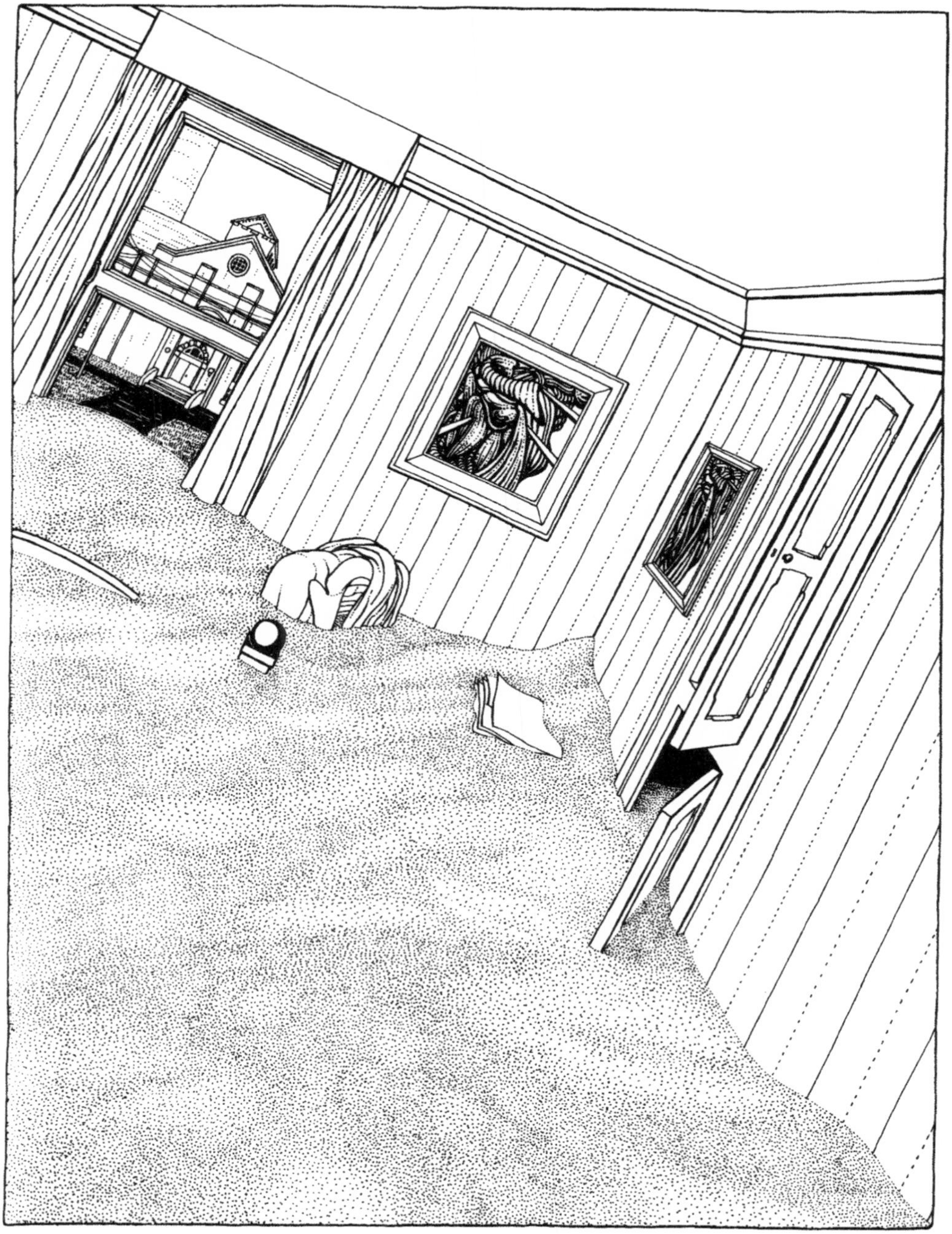

A cacophony of sound erupts ... a dense and unrelenting din ... a tangle of blasts and shrieks in which no single instrument succeeds in dominating ... either by the sheer intensity of its pitch or by the insistence of its rhythm

... but neither does this barrage of noise evolve, even for an instant, into a single sound, remaining from the outset a magnificent and ludicrous sonic convulsion in which each participle both cancels and supports the others as if its existence depended on its separation from the whole.

The symphony continues ... rising like a giant cloud of insects ... each sound a separate species, no strain omitted and none duplicated ...

collected here ... a flailing, flapping, whirring and aimlessly
directed projectile ... constantly transforming itself in wild
constellations ... above the surface of the plain ...

... constantly transforming itself in wild contortions ... as if incapable of assuming any definite (and therefore somehow vulnerable) form ...

(as if freezing of its multitude of cells into one giantic block
would render it more comprehensible ... merely because all
movement had ceased ...)

as if this sudden fixity and rigid permanence would perhaps
be more accessible ...

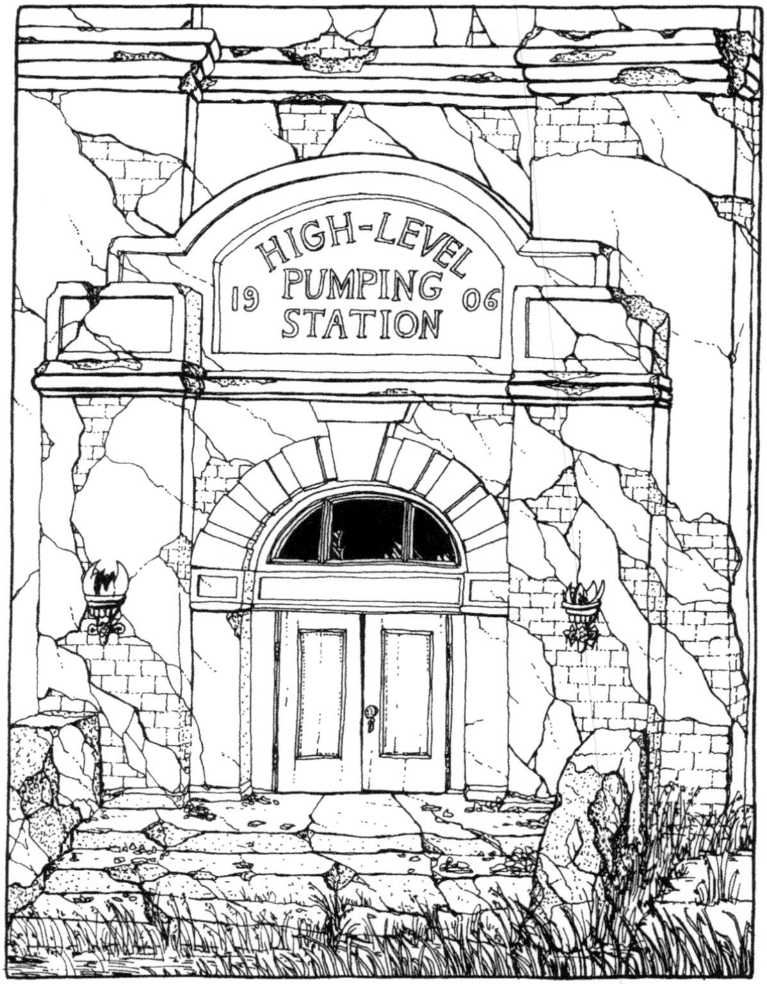
HIGH-LEVEL
19
PUMPING
06
STATION

(whereas in fact it would only prove marginally less infuriating ... its bland rigidity permitting illusions of a slow but possible advance)

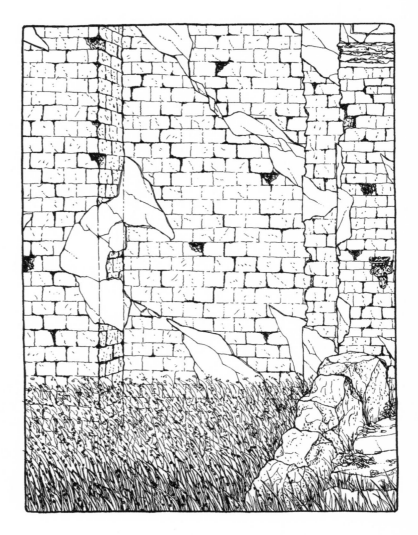

... as if in drawing closer to the stone, its inscrutable facade would conveniently collapse revealing at once and for all time ...

... or even quietly flake away in a host of thread-thin rivulets ... a million tiny cracks clicking in succession ... all seeping with the same mysterious excrement ...
... the wastage of events.

... high-level pumping station ... 1906 ... a swath of crumbling hieroglyphics ... illegible but no more ridiculous than before ... already passed over ... smeared ...

... high-level pumping station ... 1906 it gibbers plate-mouthed and cretinous ... a stick on a pile of dust.

The noise crashes on ... heaving across the page in epileptic waves ... a flood of choking retching and hysterical cries wrenched spurting from the shattered instruments with such ferocity that the air itself seemed to splinter and capitulate.

Silence.

(slight pressure on the appropriate button ... a soft click ... and all sound ceases ...)

... silence ... gradually giving way to the steady ebb and flow of breath inhaled and expelled with such laboured determination that this single activity appears to preclude all others ... including thought ...

The tape had not run out, its course (suddenly and inexplicably arrested ... its builders overtaken in their endeavour)
merely interrupted, arbitrarily blocked ... abruptly and dispassionately concluded as if all its fury had been utterly
ephemeral ... without substance or validity ... a wild baroque
ornament clinging fatuously to a now extinct idea ...

... again the breathing ...
filling the entire corridor with its insistent and depressingly
insidious undulations ... each intake an imperfect duplicate
of all those others mouldering in the void ... each expulsion
another headstone for all those yet to come ...

... *not only the jacket but the shirt as well is torn away, the buttons* (slight pressure ... and all sound ceases ...) *ripped out or sheared in two or left clinging by a thread to a fragment of material no longer attached to this writhing ... no ... this isn't right this sequence moved too fast ...*

The sound of breathing subsides ... or (more exactly) escalates to such an overwhelming volume as to appear inaudible ... freeing the ear to direct itself elsewhere to concentrate on some other noise (given that such alternatives existed) hanging hitherto unheard in this airless silent corridor.

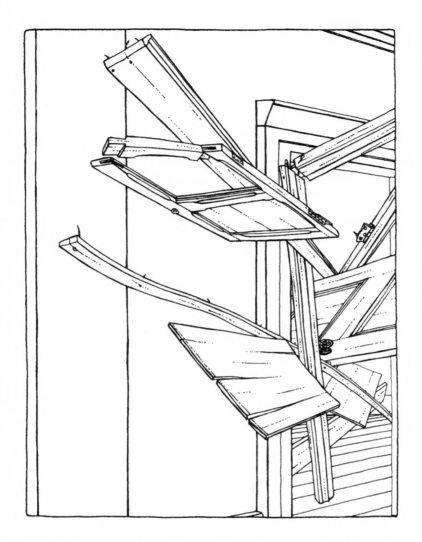

... is torn away ... ripped out ... sheared in two or left clinging
... to a fragment ... splinter ... a ragged piece of fabric

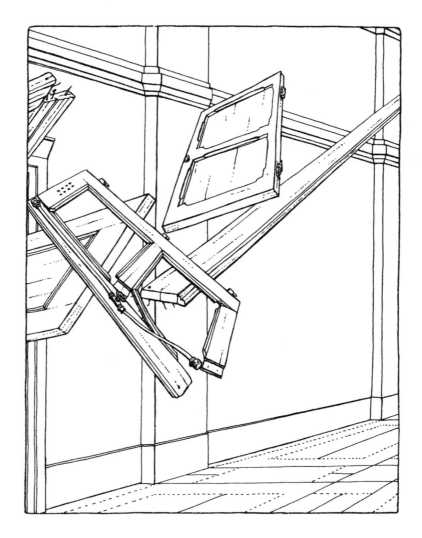

(*canvas ... paper?*) *rising on a sudden draft of air ... a useless scrap of imagery ...* barely less comprehensible than the now obliterated whole.

... again silence ...

the breathing is under control ... the spasms have been suppressed, the monotony assured ... the order, rhythm, the ritualistic progress of identical events leading to habitual conclusions ... all are as before ... guaranteed, unalterable ... a giant circle across the boards, at whose centre stands this sign, this cipher of that event.

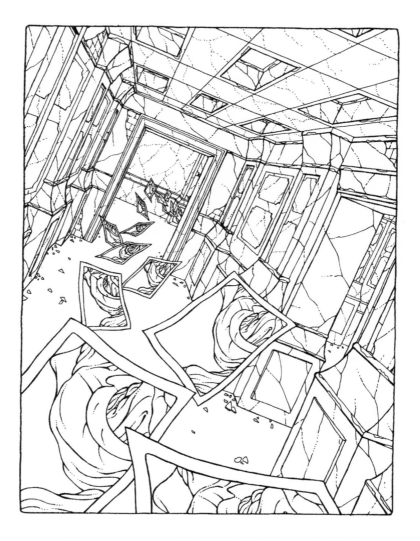

... a useless scrap ... a swirl of thin black lines slashed across the page as if this fragment had itself been further mutilated and these dark strokes were nothing more than seams ...

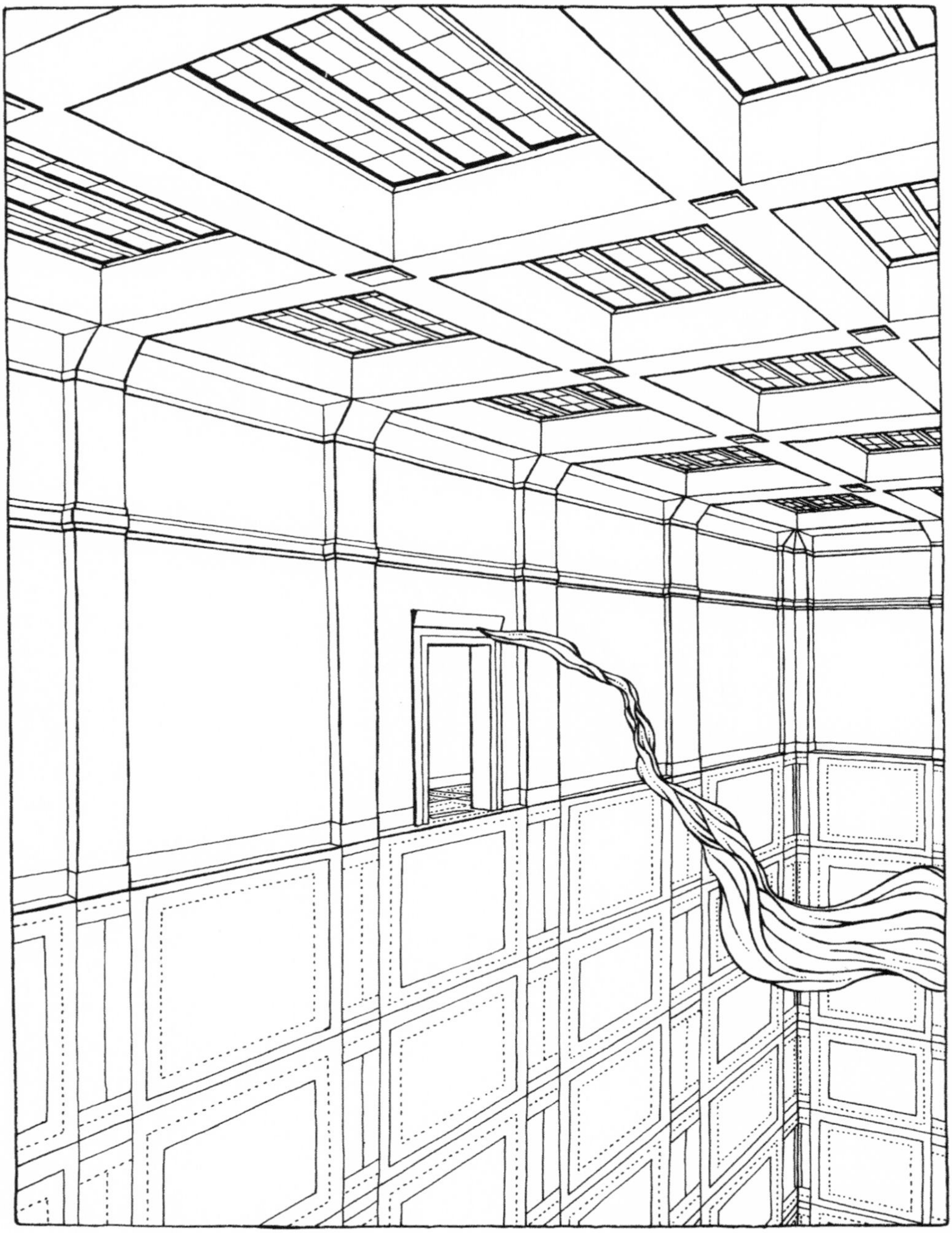

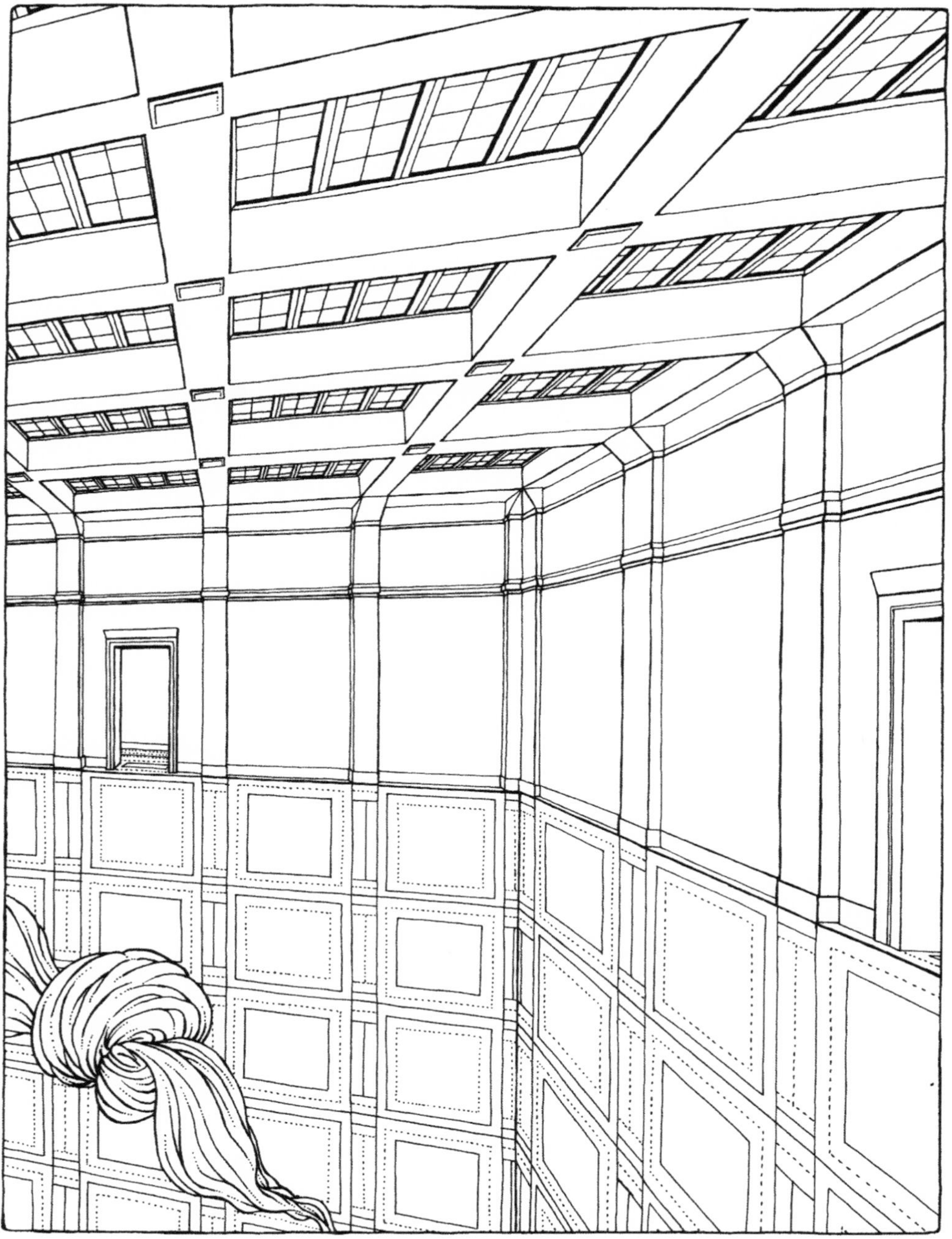

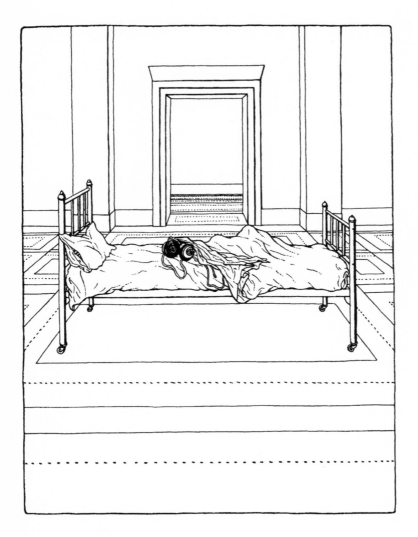

threads already faltering ...

... the sound of breath inhaled and exhaled has ceased ... the straining of the ear to retain the last faint echo of the cry is finally defeated by the violent deluge of contorted forms which bind the eye (at once blank and totally absorbed) to this rapidly deteriorating image.

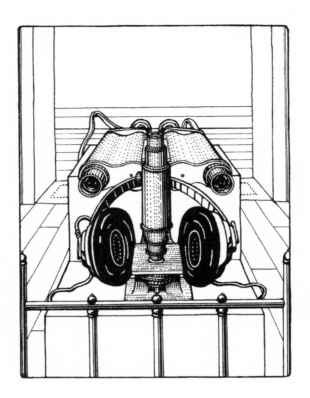

The eye and the ear alone continue their automatic functions long after (*all sound has ceased*) all configurations have been exhausted, all movements in this primordial ballet have come to rest in a stagnant pile of now unrelated particles ...

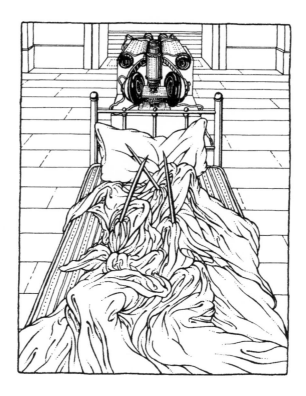

and now the eye alone ...
an interminable succession of smudged or
shattered plates (wooden frames erected one
behind the other, kept equidistant by repeated
use of metal rods, straps or cords ...) each dark
transparent lens a contradictory variation of a
single image, each variation further mutated
by reflections from those displayed on either
side ... so that the eye could now only rush on
wildly through the tunnel in the futile and
desperate hope of confronting just one opaque
and final screen ...

... no longer attached to the writhing heaving bundle of material ...

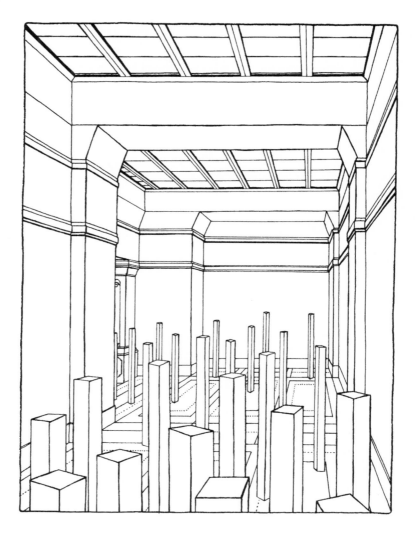

... *straining frantically against this preposterous system of cords and straps ...*

erupting yet again against that featureless facade ...
repeating all its infinite convulsions slowly, as if each tiny
splash had been halted in its course, pinned down, examined
and dissected ...

its flight meticulously recorded in the hope that, when assembled, these fluctuating observations would somehow serve to reconstruct and ultimately illuminate that thing whose very nature defied examination ...

The cage stood as before ...

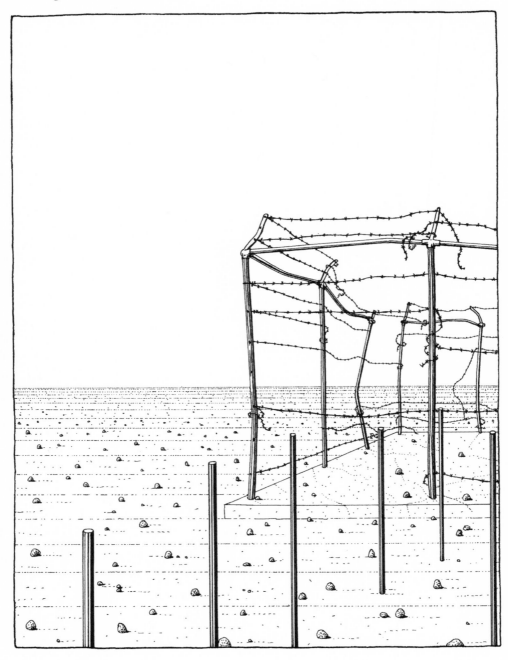

... immune to chaos and decay.

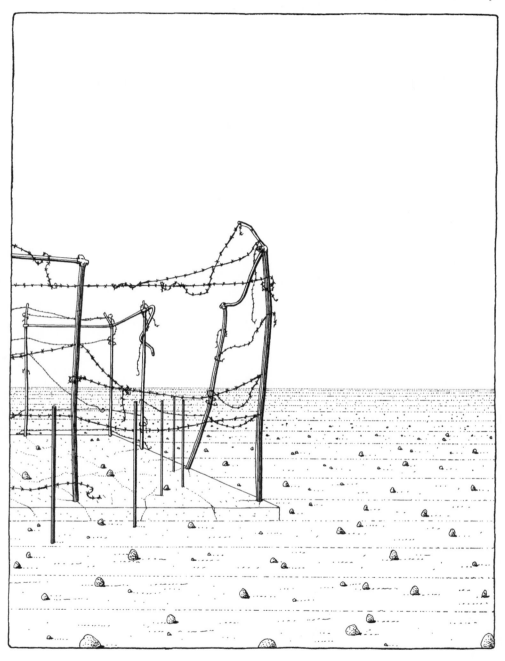

... system of metal rods, cords and weights elaborately suspended within a rigid wooden framework bolted firmly in the centre of the floor.

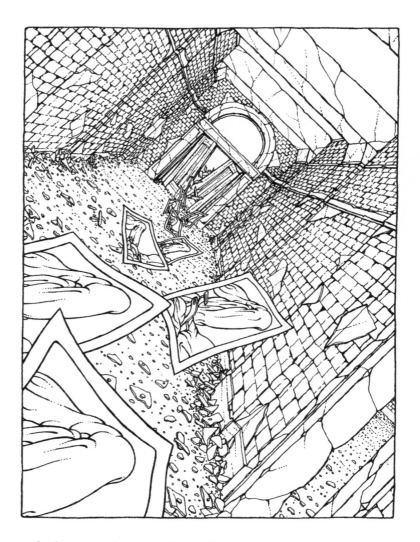

... kicking out desperately amid this momentary hesitation ...
this mounting indecision ... (all which had been so carefully
planned in every detail now, for an instant, seemed invalid,
absurd and, worse still, irrelevant)

... wooden framework skilfully constructed with a craftman-
ship almost excessively meticulous considering the brutality
of its purpose ... all joints precisely dove-tailed (where nails
would suffice), reinforced with polished metal plates
(square, as always) (themselves engraced with labyrinthine
patterns) and all its surfaces lacquered like a gleaming,
brittle sheath ...

less an actual machine than an odd and enigmatic abstraction, totally unnatural, its utility obscured and isolated from the encroaching vegetation ...

the entire apparatus (beams, plates, cords, straps, weights, rivets, rods and stones) frozen at a terrifying angle, propped up at one corner by the poles, balanced diagonally between the ceiling and the floor ...

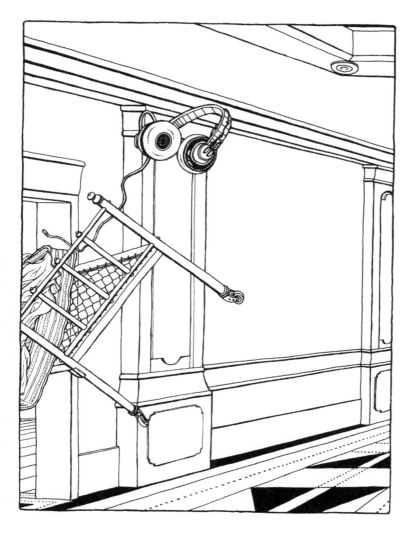

as if it had been hurled across the room and, for no apparent reason, arrested in its flight ... rescued from its inevitable, shattering descent and subsequent collapse

held in this peculiar position ...

as if outside the laws of physics ... as if the room itself was
at fault, its gravity displaced, its geometry illusionistic ...

its perspectives all distorted, its unfinished decoration in danger of slipping

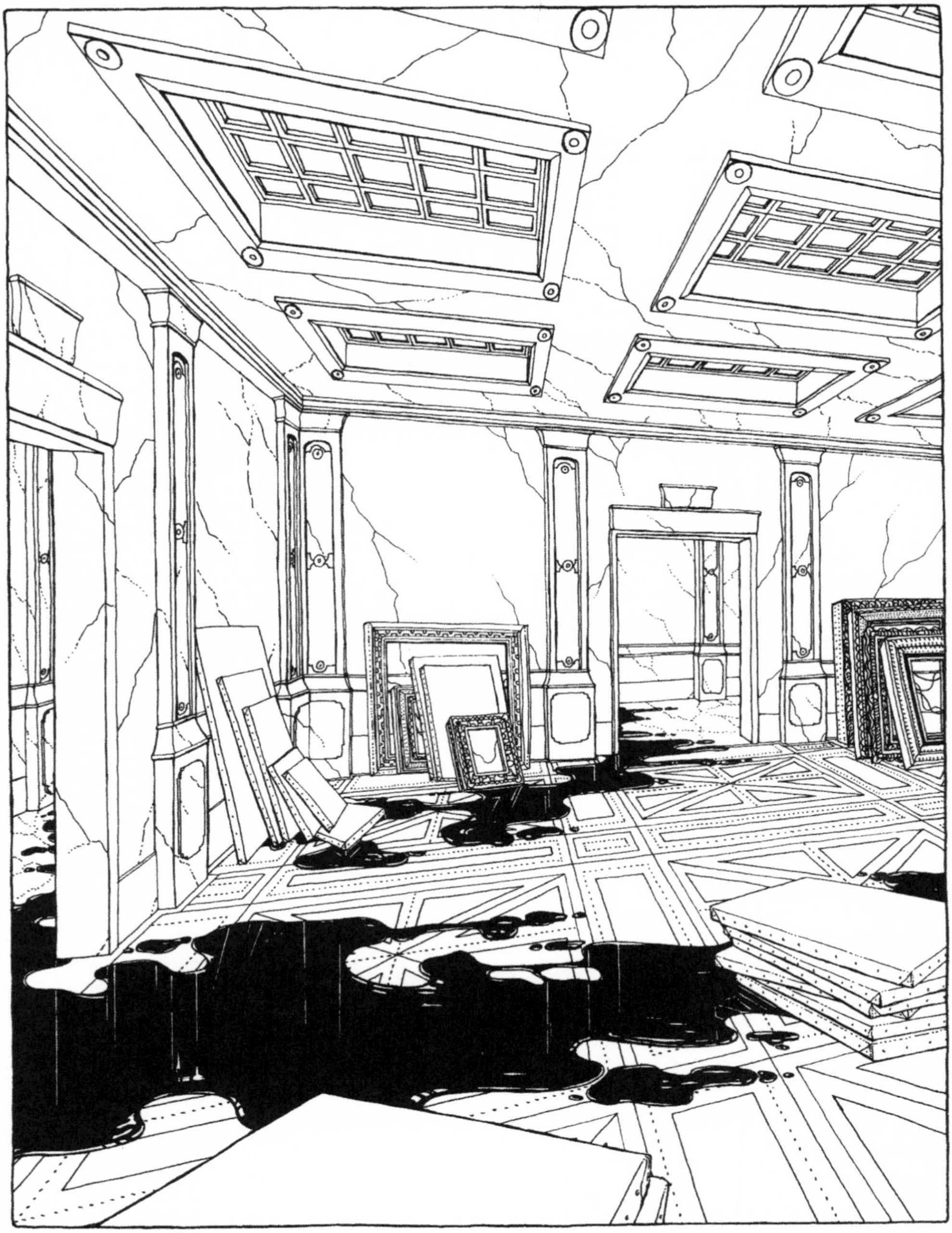

beneath the eye to hurtle wildly across the crumbling walls

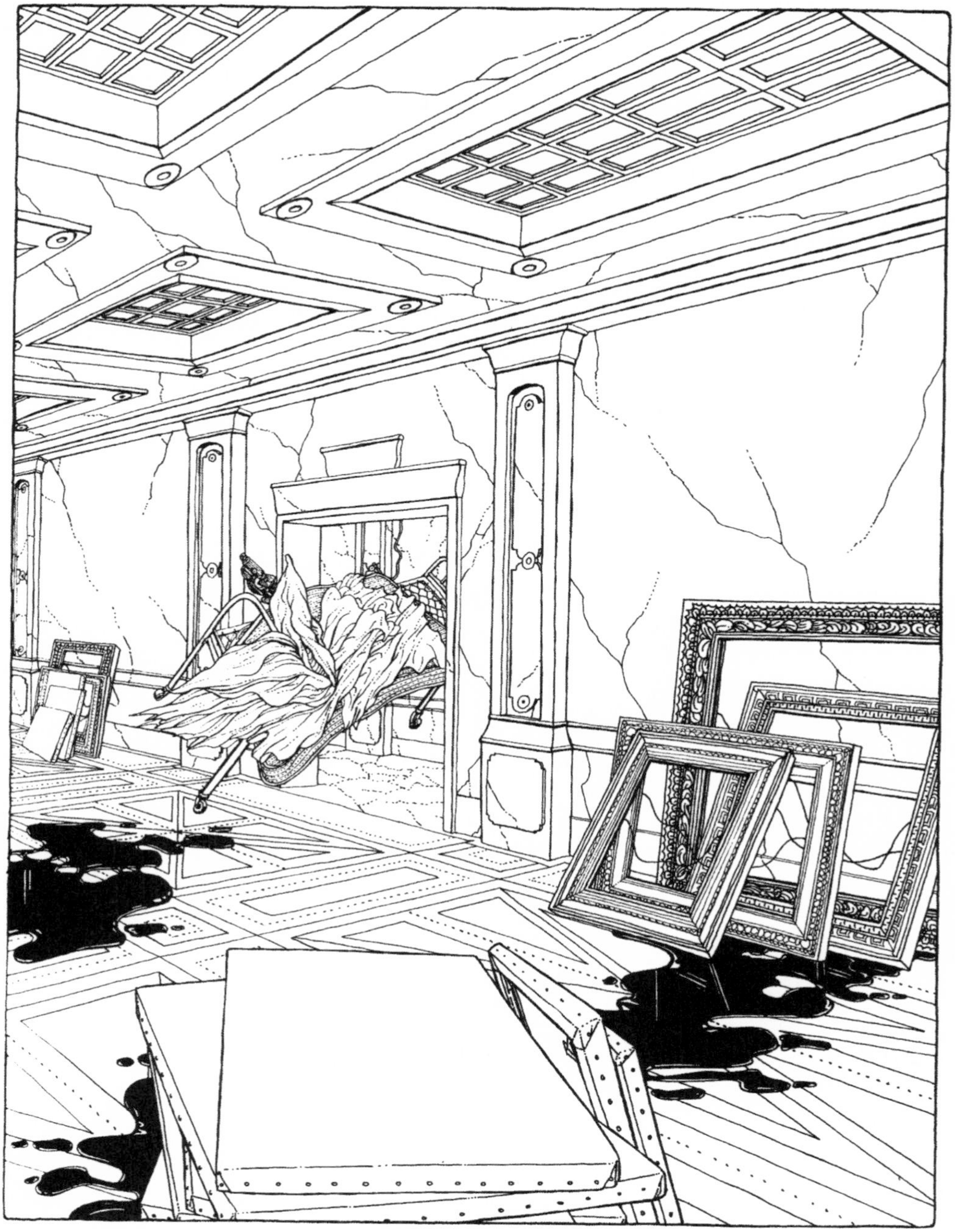

But in here, *after all this ... what?*
A few familiar forms ... props arranged theatrically across the painted floor ... stagnating in utility ... remote, banal and unconvincing ... concealing beneath their fractured surfaces ...

... a few additional elements (or so it would appear) ... but basically the scene remains unchanged ... always the same slow and silent drama (a magician's act caught just before its fascinating and predictable conclusion by some anonymous photographer seated in the audience) suspended across a glossy sheet ... the fold along its centre, now, long after the event ...

infinitely more real than this remnant of that perpetually unfinished trick.

cords, weights, metal spikes and all the other obscene paraphernalia stacked obsessively and catalogued according to
obtuse criteria ... the spikes equated with the cords (*binding
tighter, penetrating deeper* than in the original scenario), the
metal plates filed carefully with the unmarked sheets, the
assorted fragments of material, the scraps of canvas (paper?)
ripped away from the splintered frames, the frames themselves studded at irregular intervals with bent or rusted nails
...

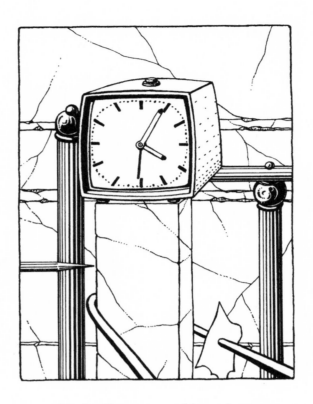

No ... this is all wrong ... this entire sequence is moving far too slowly ... the objects have still not been displaced ... they are all still grouped in categories in the centre of the drum (which has only just commenced rotating on its axis) ... each revolution of this cylinder seems almost interminably long and the narrow aperture through which the lens protrudes restricts investigation to an absolute minimum. Inevitably the speed will increase (in fact it is already doing so, imperceptibly) ... for the moment it will crawl with laboured regularity like the hour hand across ...

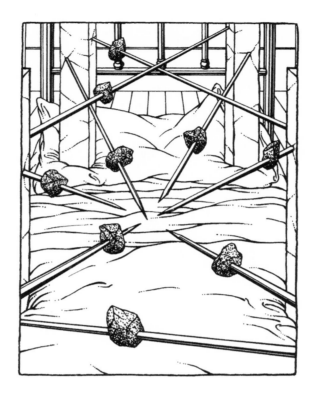

the unmarked face of a giant clock at whose
centre is grouped ...

The drum has only just been set in motion. As
it gathers speed, the objects grouped around
its fulcrum will be displaced ... the scraps of
fabric, paper will be the first to move (having
insufficient density to resist the outward pull),
jerked from their original positions by the
artificial gravity of the machine ... fluttering
in spasmodic leaps like wounded (wingless,
crippled) insects until they reach, by ever
more erratic paths, the outer, endless wall,
where they remain transfixed, their writing
limbs all pointing inward.

The lens pierces the wall through a very
narrow opening. It is bolted in a fixed position, allowing no lateral movement whatso-
ever. It can, however, focus telescopically,
permitting intimate (and detached) observa-
tion of the activities of only those insects
thrown within its immobile glaring circle.
Thus the drama unfolds piecemeal ... always
incomplete and (since its range excludes the
very centre of the cylinder) ultimately
invalid, absurd and, worse still, irrelevant.

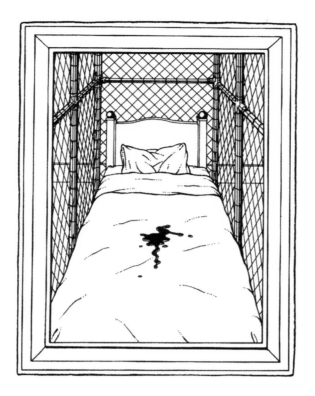

Directly opposite the lens, painted on the
concave wall, is a window, to the left of which
runs a vertical black line (representing,
perhaps, the corner of the room) ... to the left
again of this line is another painted area, this
time in imitation of a door. Following the wall
in the opposite direction (starting from the
window) another black line is reached, after
which another door (or rather two doors, set
one above the other ... obviously a cupboard
in the wall). Right in front of the window,
extending across the entire floor toward the
spy-hole, is the bed.

The sheets are wrenched backward, thrust away in a jagged arabesque ... deep furrows splay outward from the knot in a broken and irregular spiral ... one corner, free of cords and weights, billows up for an instant and collapses in a crumpled heap ...

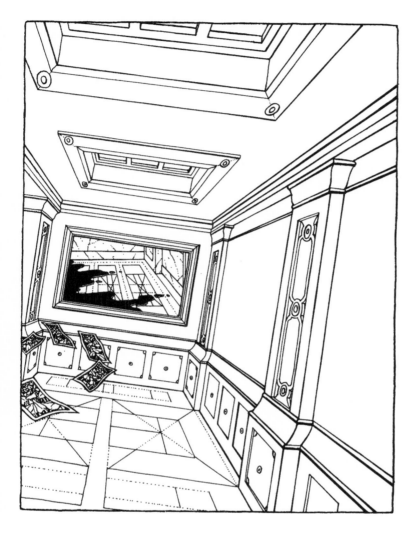

The breathing accelerates ... a rush of air sucked in and almost instantly expelled (as if the air itself were acid) ... *the creases in the shirt* (stained and eaten by the fluid) *rise and fall quite visibly ...*

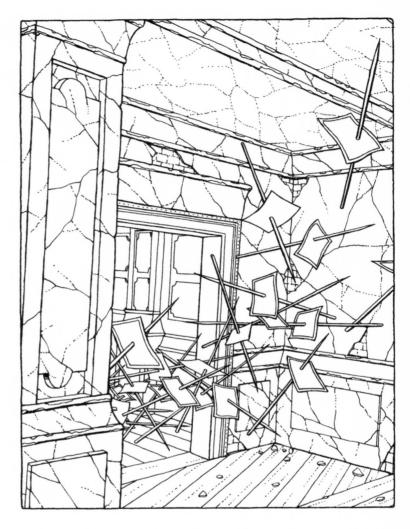

... the folds, running laterally across the bundle ... echoing the movement of the sheets ...

caught up swept away as the entire flapping, flailing pile is dragged across the spikes and sucked on down the corridor ...

… *the cord* … loosely entwined around the limp bundle …

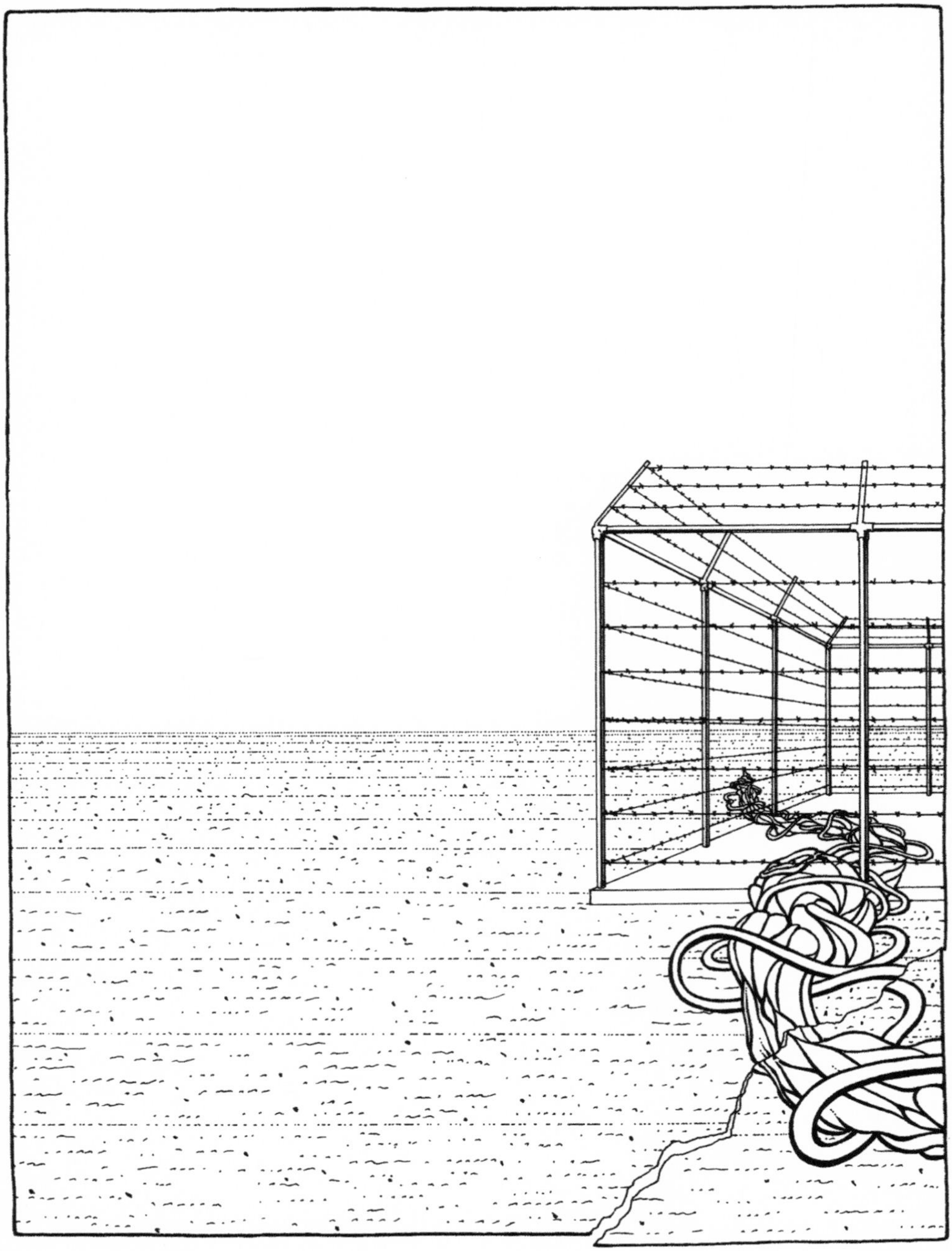

trailing uselessly across the defaced image of the cage ...

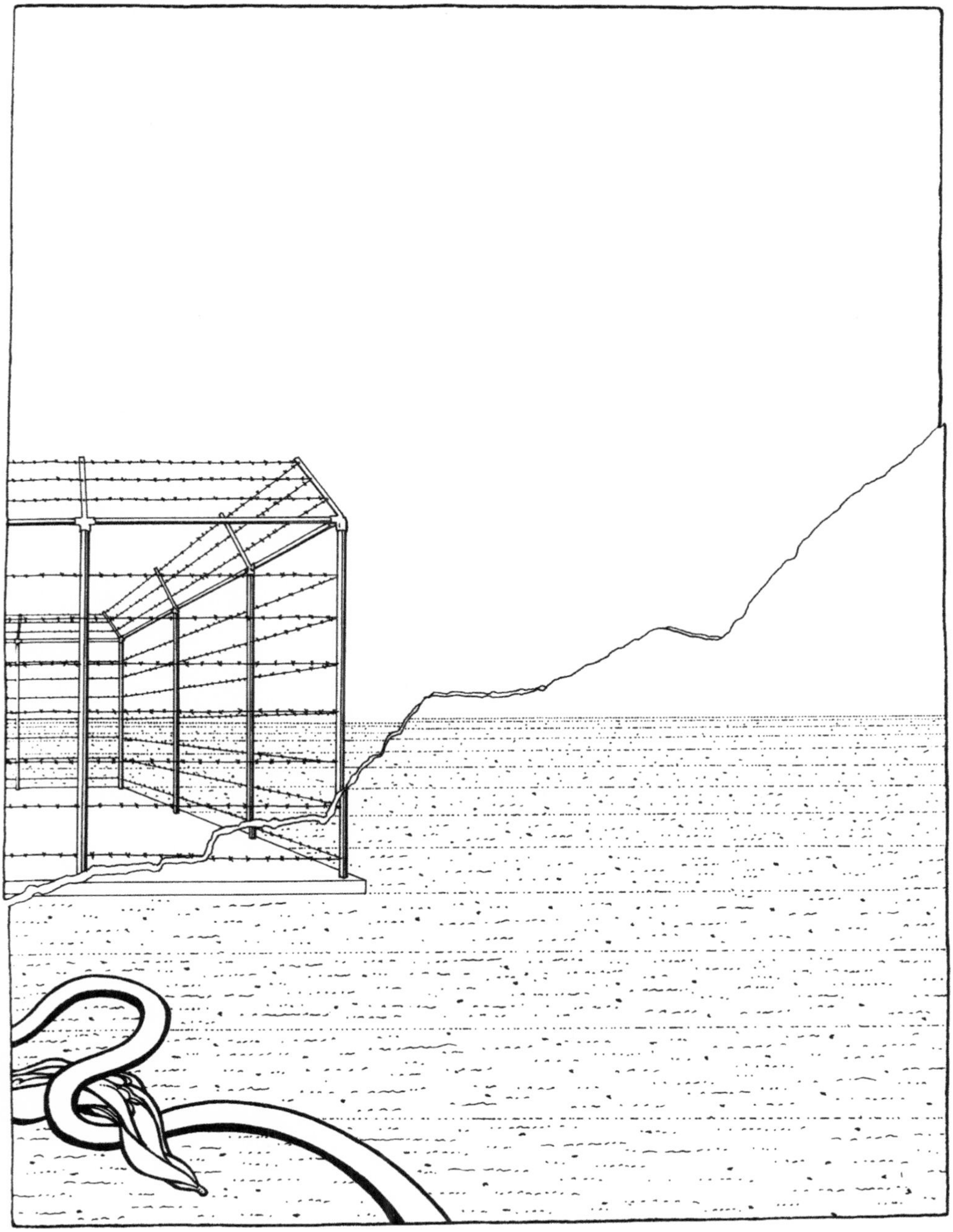

... silence ...
the single grating sound of paper torn erratically in two ...
... a pause ...
the same sound repeated ... but with a minute alteration ...
a tiny escalation at the climax of the rip ...

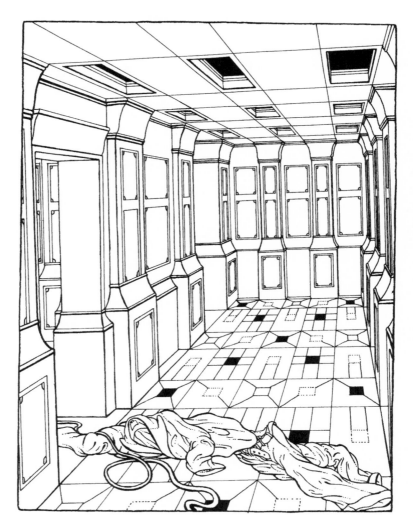

Silence again.

... this time a longer pause ...

then the rip once more ... again a variation ... now a much longer interval ... followed finally by a rapid succession of near identical repetitions of the sound ... as if ...

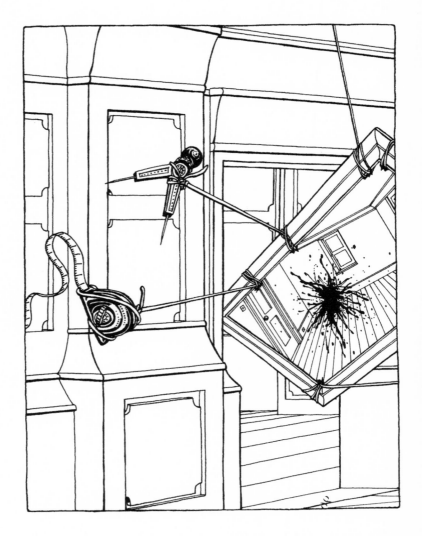

... as if reducing all these sheets to fragments would annul the reality of that thing whose existence could never be recorded accurately anyway ...

as if this stack of papers (each sheet already rendered obso-
lete by those which follow) could ever have been definitive
... each carnivorous image feeding on the sum of all the
others which have gone before.

... *but the noise crashes on* ... all instruments (if that is what they are)

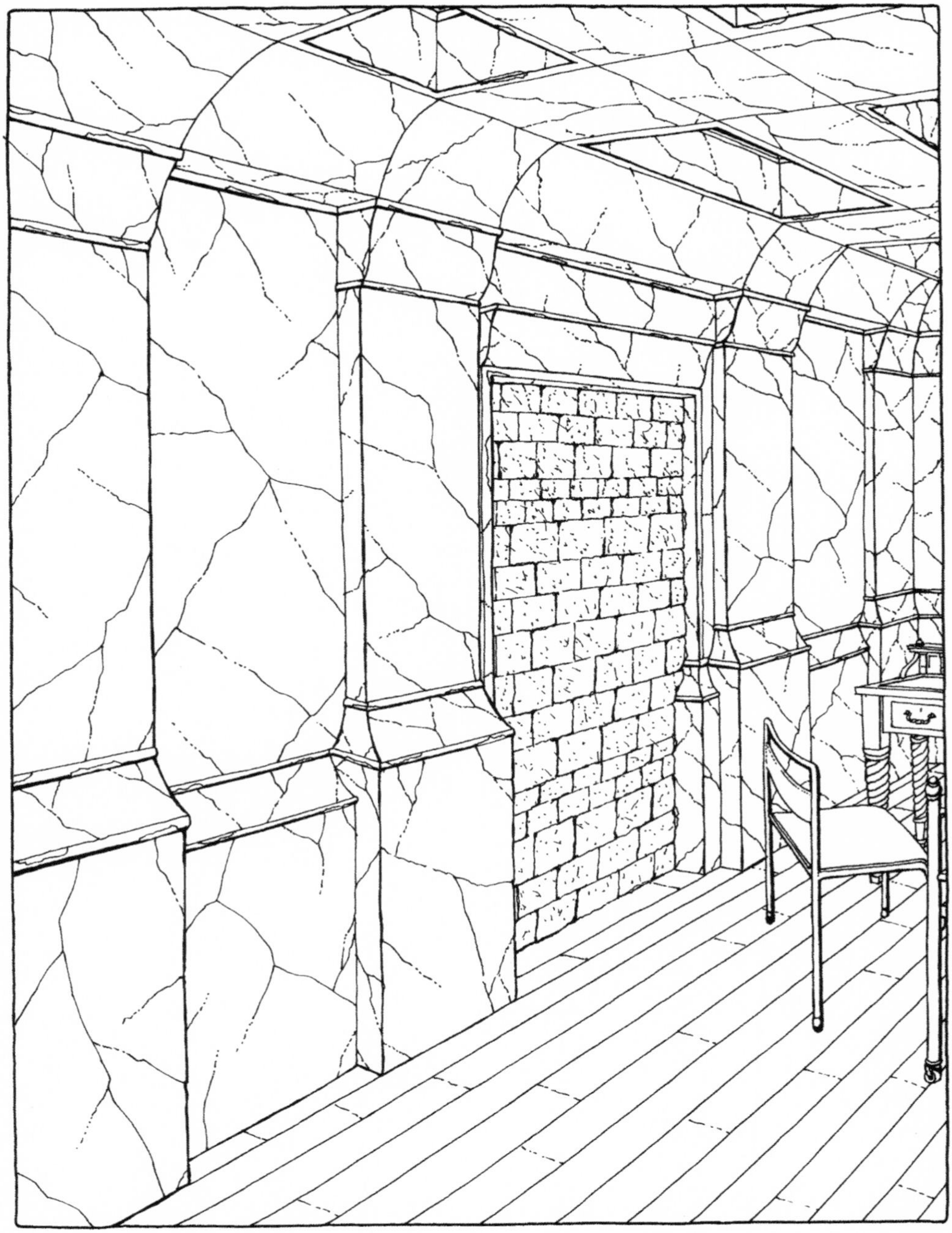

screaming out at random (and in unison) their repertoire of shrieks ...

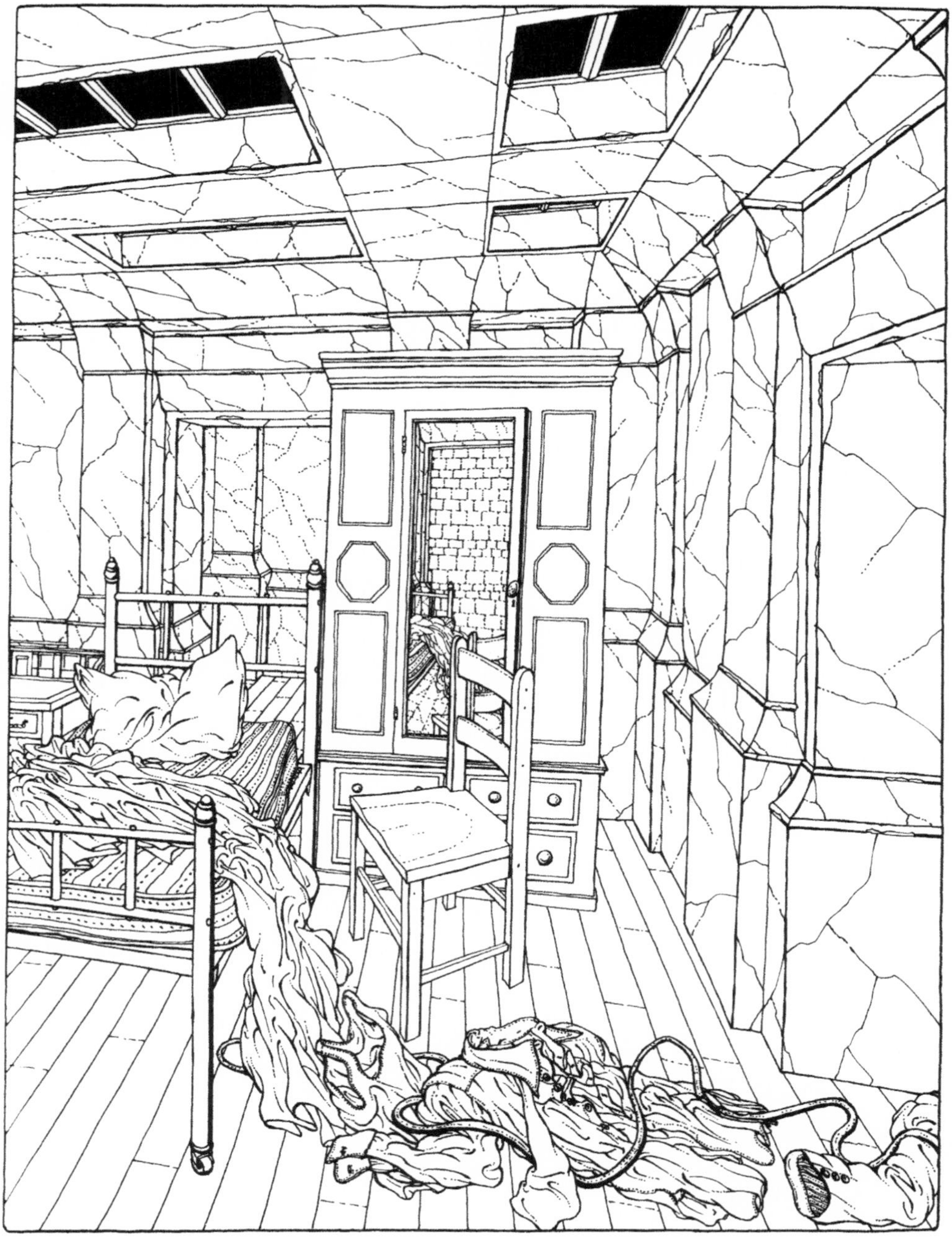

... the air above the plain, a solid sheet of grotesque, hybrid sounds,

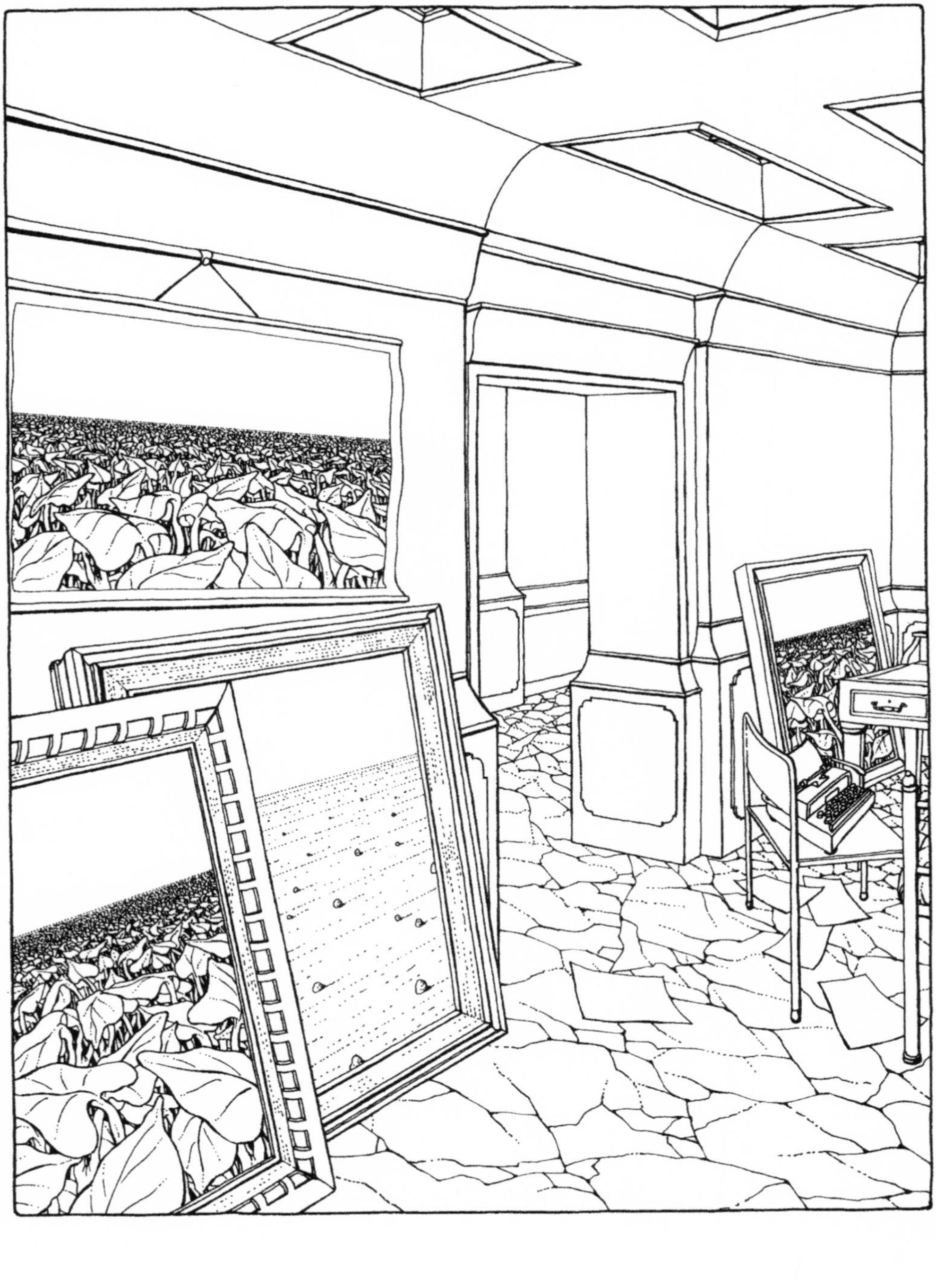

a hideous suspended parody of the vegetation underneath.

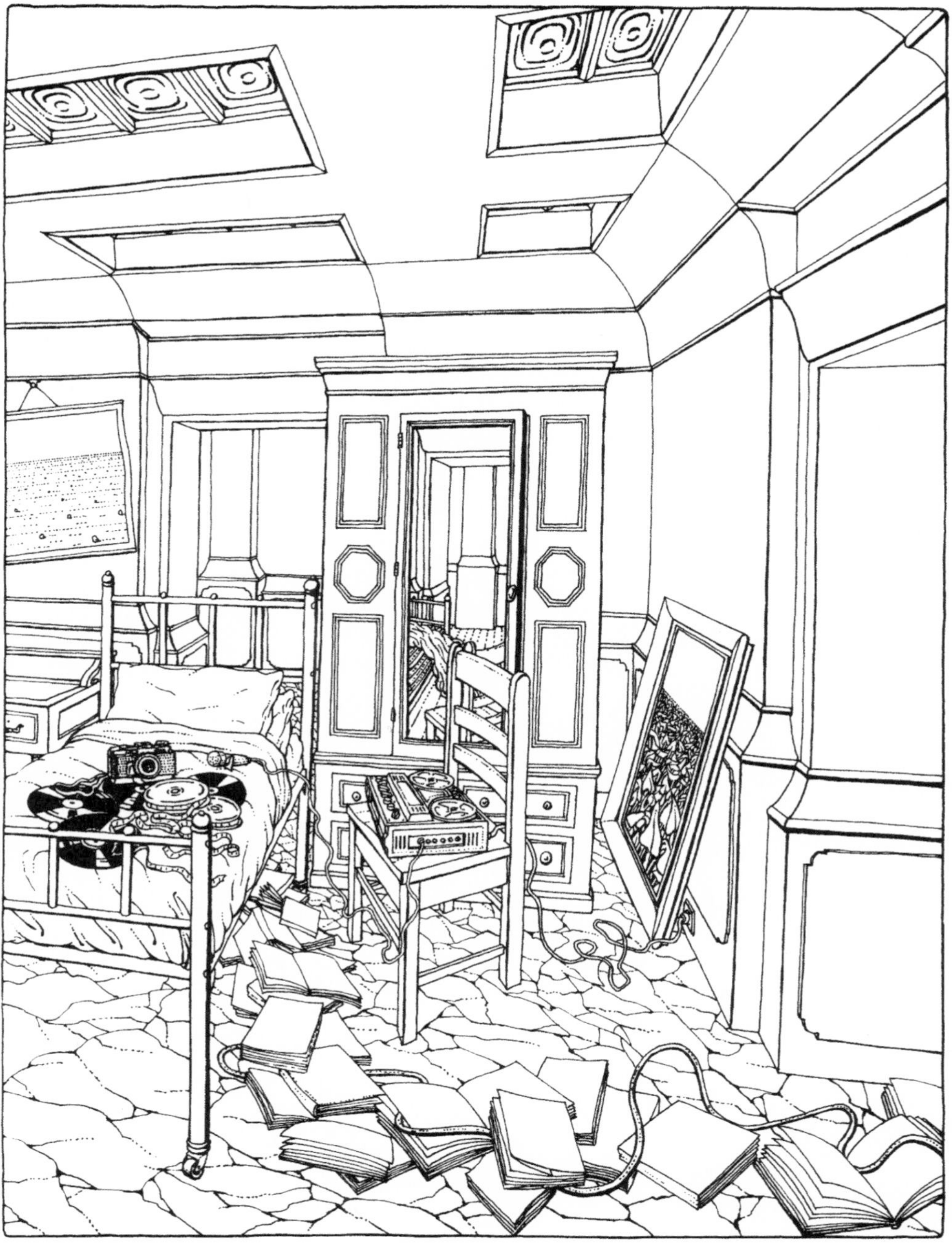

But now the stain has spread too far, the fluid has begun its irreversible attack upon the fabric, the rot and mould are slowly devastating every scrap of paper ...

(whether discarded as inadequate or hoarded away for some obscure eventual purpose) ... the lens, shuddering uncontrollably, is ...

The lens is carefully concealed within the lamp, installed in place of the missing light bulb, with the result that illumination in that part of the room is somewhat limited. Also limited is the range of this intruding eye.

The lamp, screwed onto the wall directly above the bed, extends slightly over the bedstead at such an angle as to make it impossible to record any activity that might take place at the very head of this truncated mattress.

The pillow, then, is completely obscured from view (which may or may not be a matter of significance). Thus within this rigid circle are perceived, in turn, the remainder of the bed (with all its encumbrances) the painted doors on either side (one, on the left, ajar ... escape?) (the other two ... the cupboard ... closed), two vertical black lines (denoting perhaps the edges of the picture frame), and finally the painting itself (of a window) hanging in the centre of the wall, directly opposite the lamp.

The window is quite bare ... neither curtains nor blinds ... perhaps not even panes of glass (it is hard to tell since no stylized equivalent of reflection has been attempted) ... in fact, apart from the window frame itself, nothing obstructs the view into the cylinder which (fortunately) is very brightly lit, perhaps from the lamp fixed onto the wall across the other side. The cylinder is almost completely empty ... none of the usual debris is in evidence ... only one object commands attention ... bolted firmly in the centre of the floor ... the cage ...

... the cage stands as before, that is to say, immaculately preserved ... each of its twelve steel posts glistening under the yellow light as if they had each been (only moments before?) polished to accentuate their brutal verticality. The eleven horizontal bars are painted black, and hanging from them at regular intervals are the straps, ten of them ... nine stripped of the massive iron buckle which terminates the last, the one stretched out across the floor until it almost reaches the single, concave wall of this empty cylinder ...

... the cylinder itself has only just begun its revolutions ... as it gathers speed the objects grouped around its fulcrum assume, collectively ... *no* ... as it gathers speed the whole intricate system of cords, weights, metal spikes and rods, brass plates engraved with labyrinthine patterns, bricks, scraps of fabric, paper, canvas, unmarked sheets ... the entire elaborate network of components begins to shudder into wild spasmodic motion, rattling almost farcically within the framework of the machine.

The machine hangs suspended by the cords and straps at an almost terrifying angle. It is prevented from either swaying or rotating by the careful placement of eight wooden rods or poles, each of different length depending on the distance to be covered from the floor to the most accessible portion of the framework. Between these unequal spokes, beneath the whole grotesque contraption (on the hub) has been placed, once more, the bed ... its four sides exactly parallel to the four walls of this otherwise deserted room.

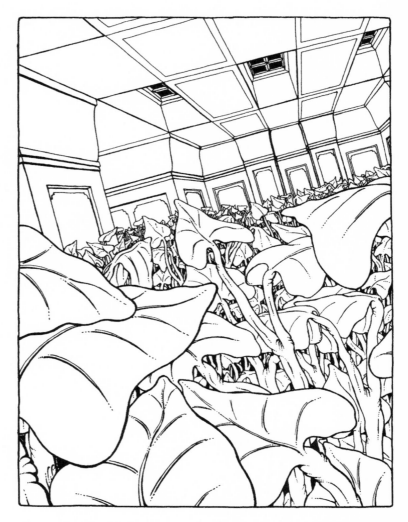

The vegetation has risen to the second level of the panelling and extends the entire length of the corridor ... presumably around the corner as well ... the three small skylights in the ceiling have been blacked out ... either that or it is night ...

... the leaves, all very similar in shape, vary in size depending on their supposed distance from the picture plane. The stems and branches are long and slender, thickening slightly at their wrinkled joints ... the impression is of artificiality (accentuated, perhaps, by the stylized treatment used throughout).

... the foliage has disappeared completely. The corner has been reached. The masonry and plasterwork are in an advanced stage of delapidation. No details of the panelling remain ... in fact it is difficult to see where such decoration would have been ...

... the end wall particularly is quite different in structure, the two buttresses having been removed entirely to accommodate the painting (of the doorway and a portion of the facade ... disastrously decayed) ... scraps and fragments of plaster are scattered across the floor ... bricks, cracked and chipped, fill the air ...

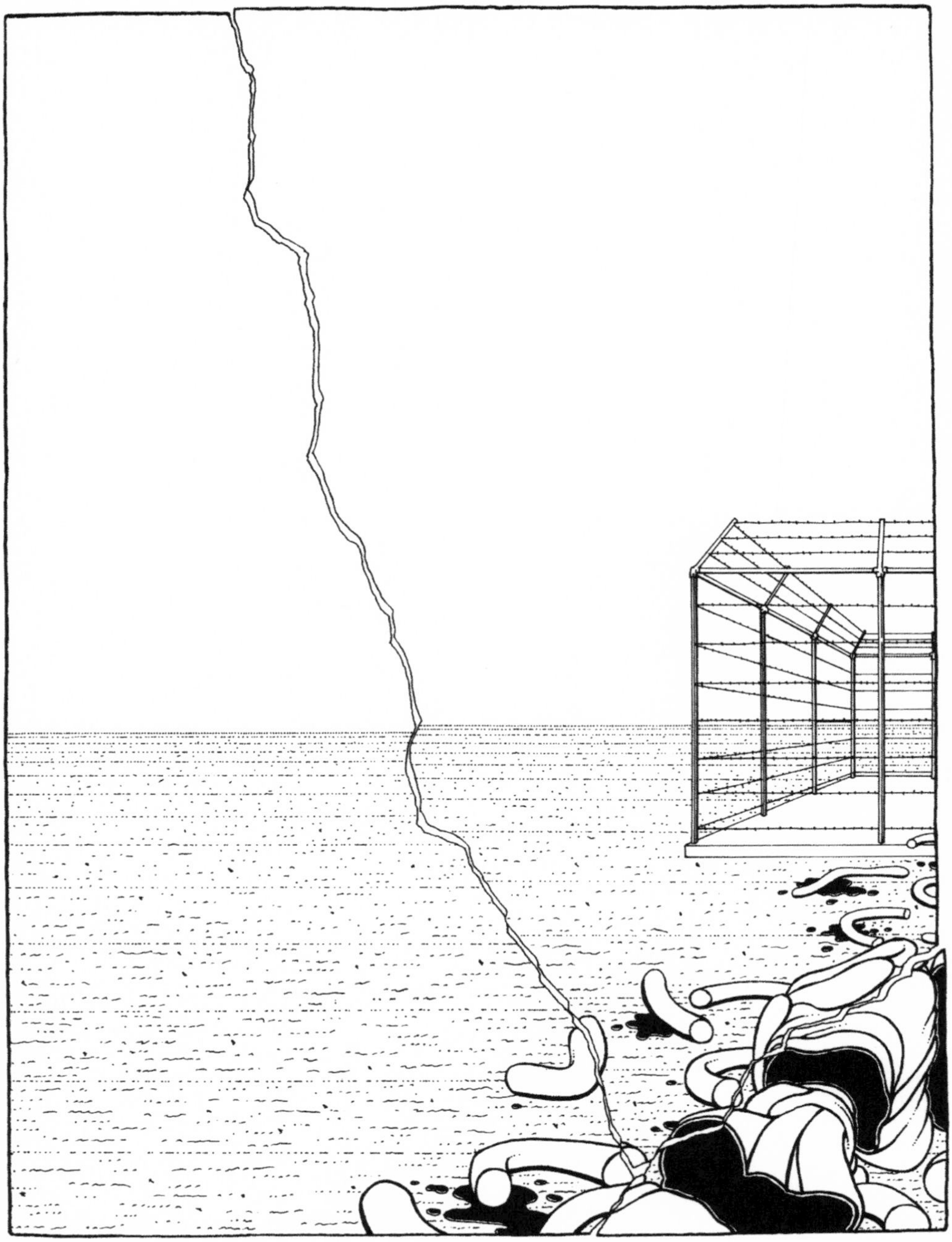

... fill the air ...

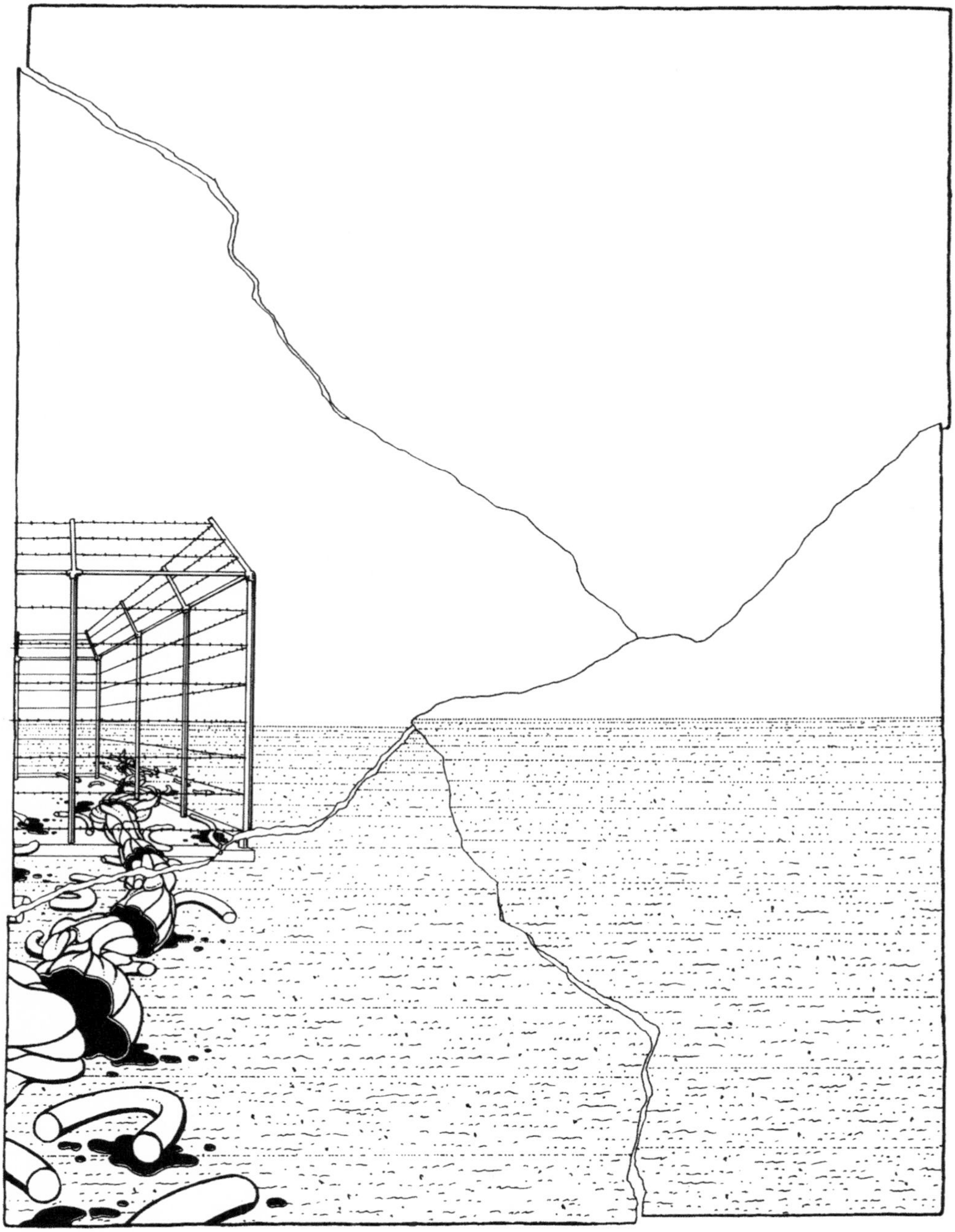

... bricks, cracked and chipped ... seven ... standing in the fluid on top of columns stained with rivulets ... lying in the spattered liquid which has defaced this trail of screens placed or thrown or fallen across the checkered floor.

The corridor, much shorter than the others, reduced in height and stripped of all but a minimum of decoration ... the room ... just visible through the central doorway ... and again the usual accessories ...

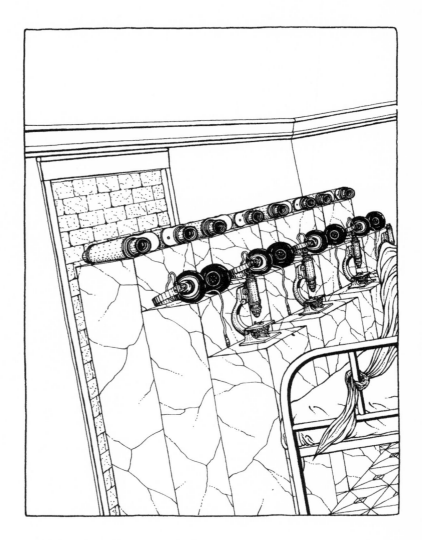

... all movement has terminated ...
... all sound has ceased ...
... all permutations are finished, all variations played out
... all fragments have come to rest and all surfaces have been restored
... all exits ...

The air within the room, a damp transparent mould, settles like a sheath around the objects, its porous underbelly draining them of any singularity, reducing everything to one, single bland, continuous, oppressive surface ...

... the machine hangs uselessly between the ceiling and the floor

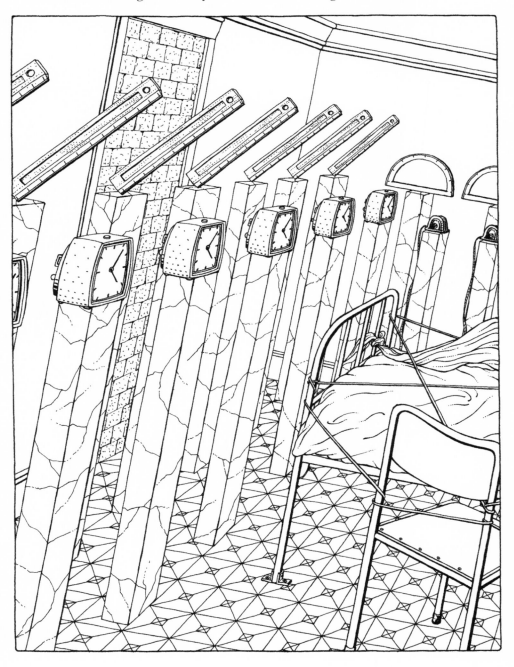

... suspended in a giant block of glass at the moment of its collapse

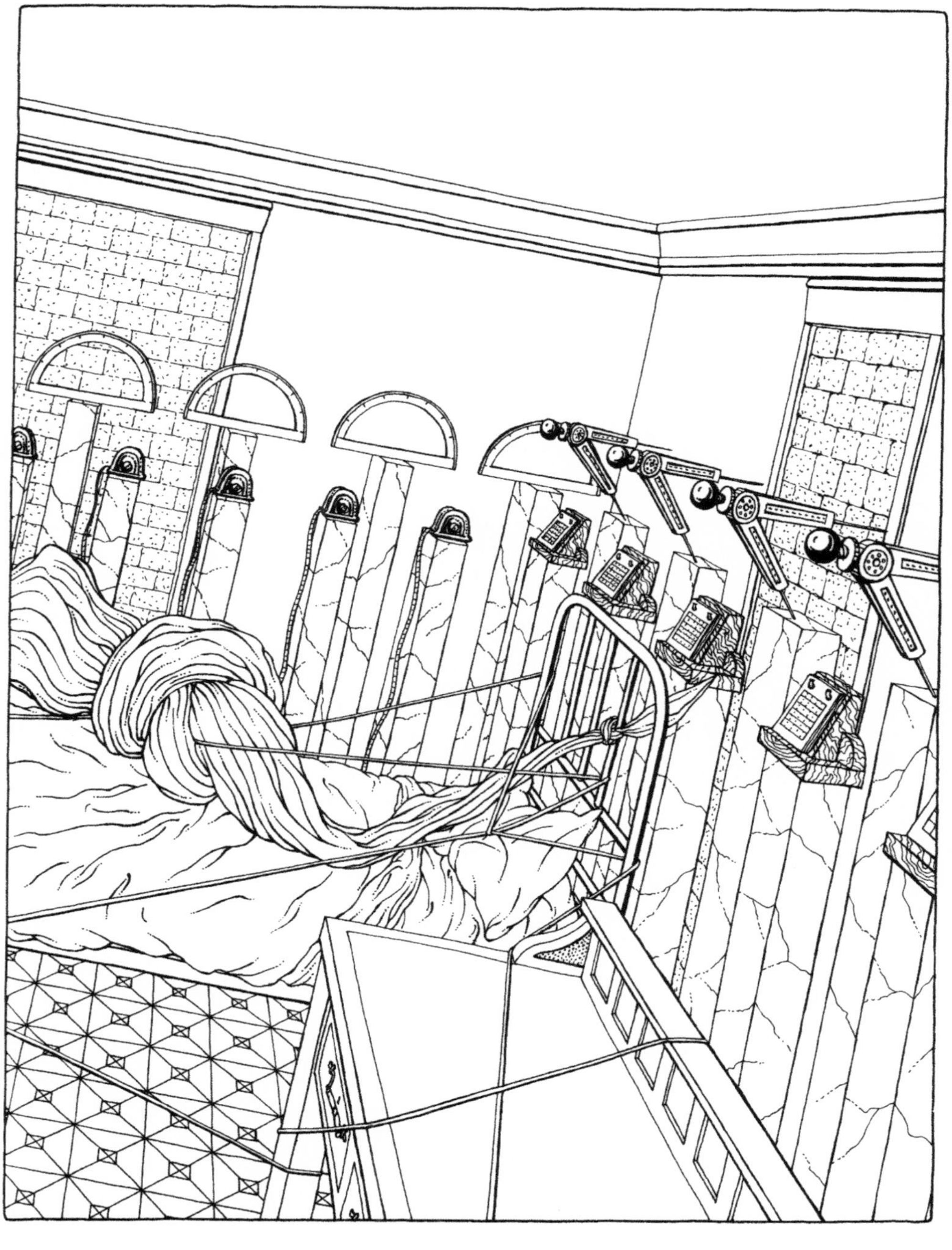

... at its core, the cylinder too is poised between rotations ...

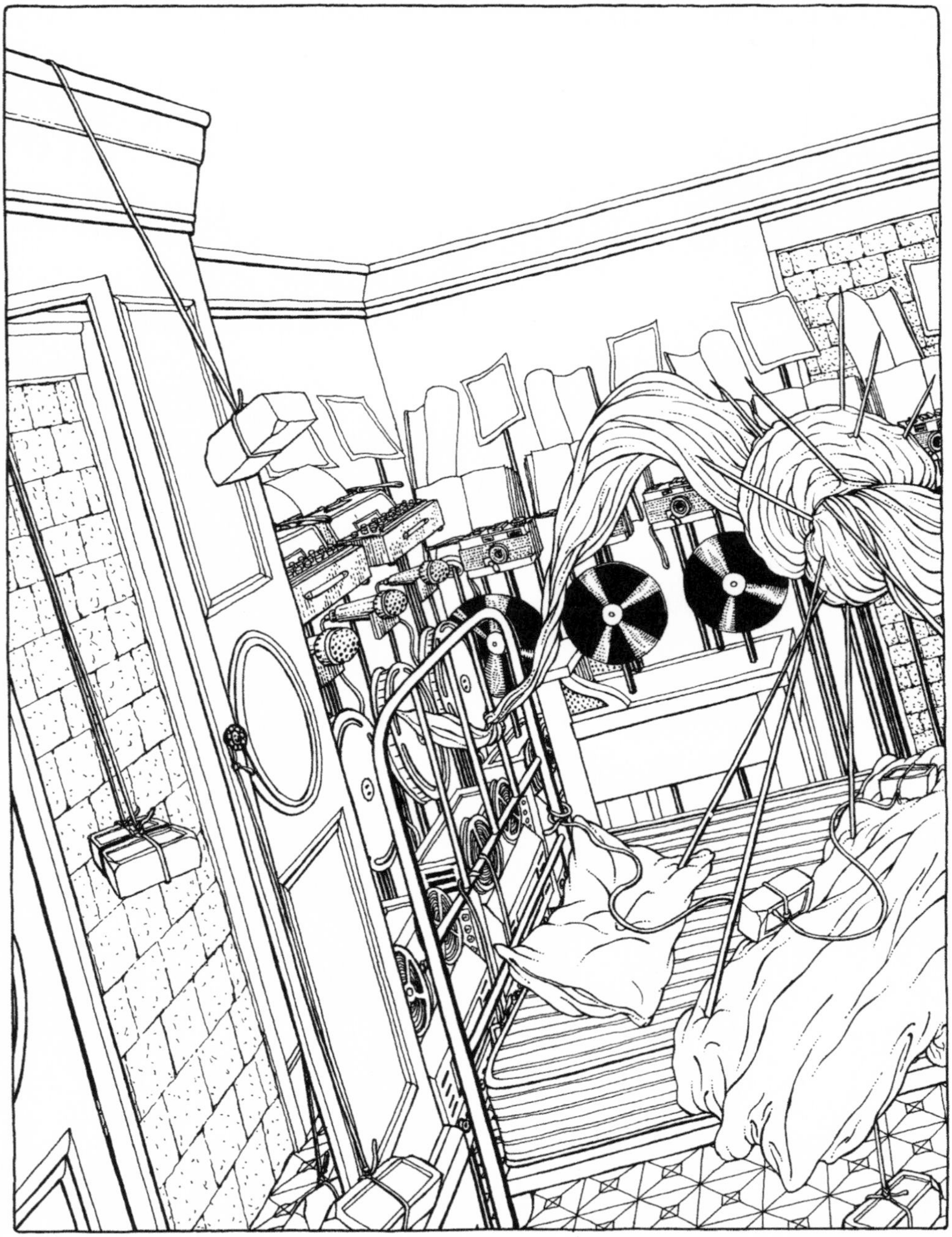

transfixed upon its waste, within the monotony of its wall ...

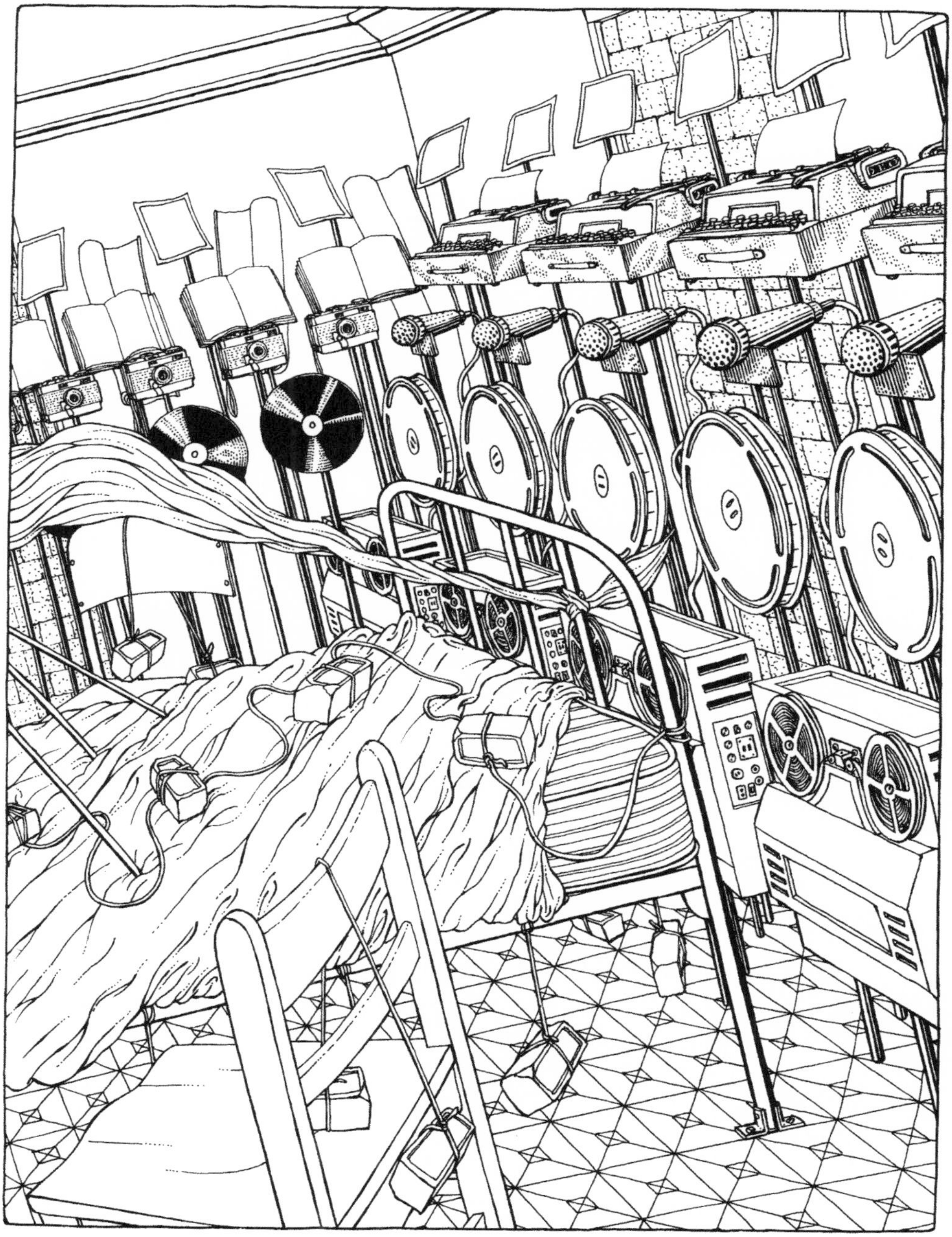

... only one object still commands attention ...

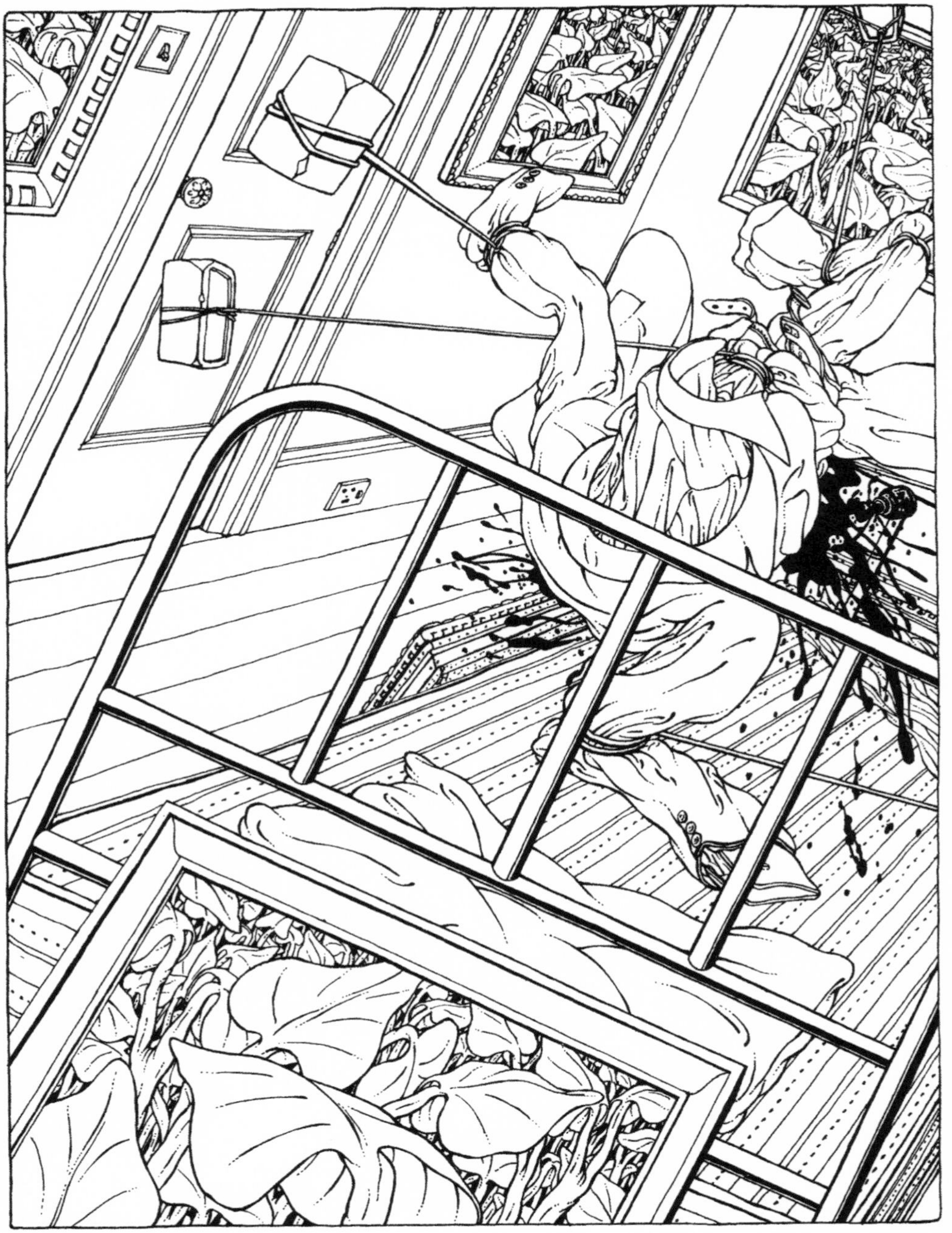

... rooted firmly in the centre of the plain ...

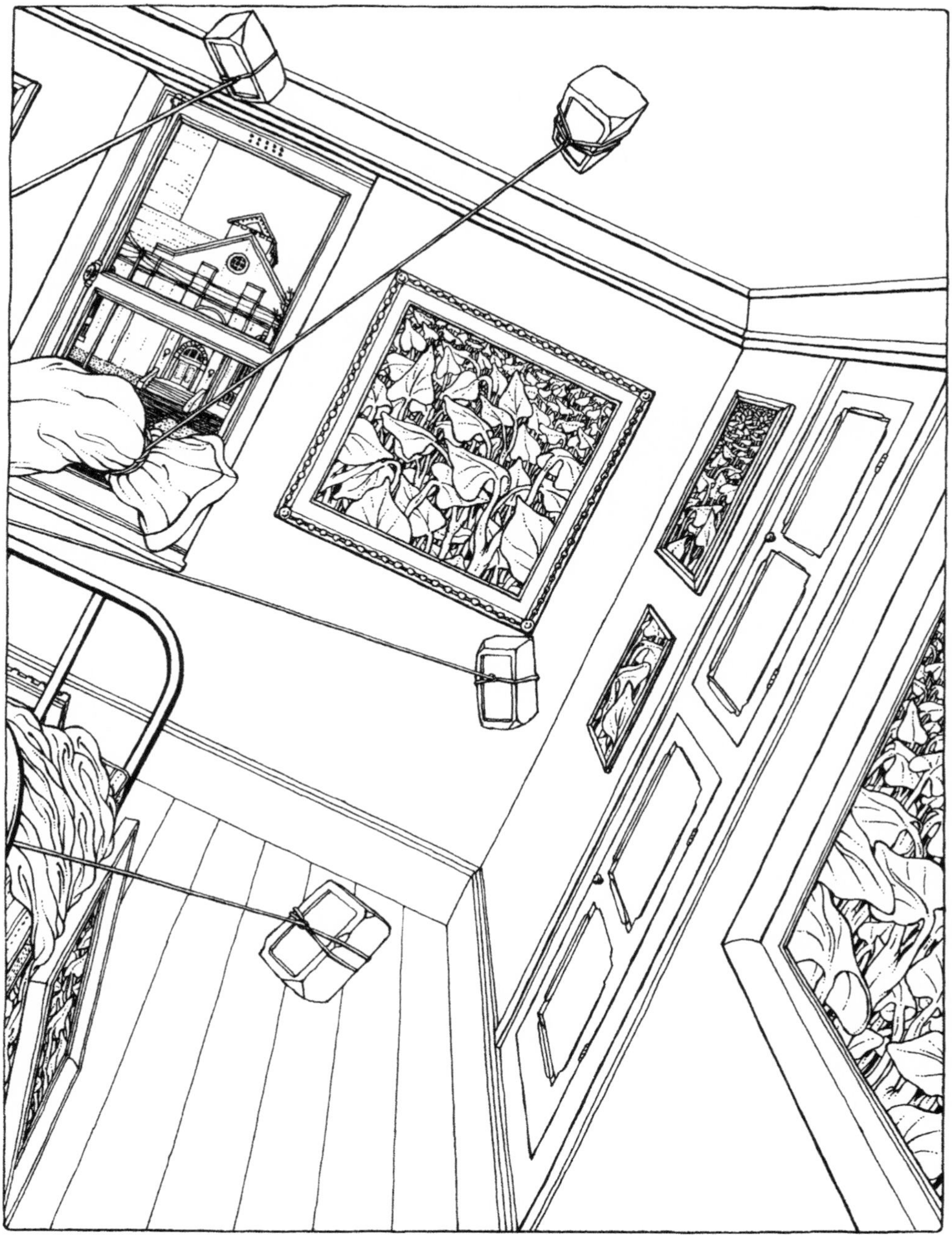

... the cage ...

... the cage ...

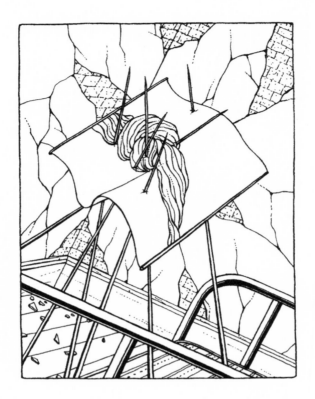

... a tangle of truncated opaque screens repeating its convulsions

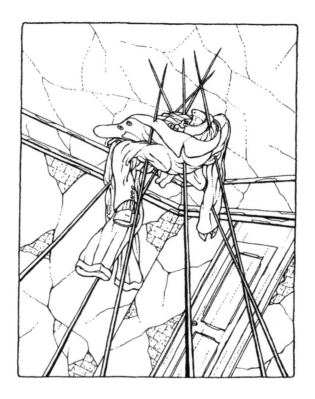

... a possible advance into choking retching and hysterical silence

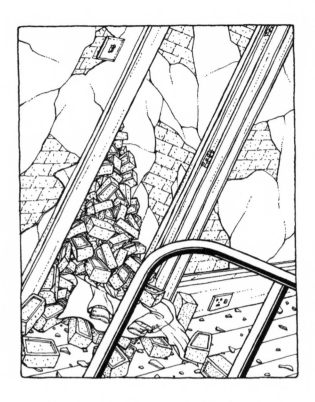

... dispassionately concluded and torn away
... hanging mute defeated

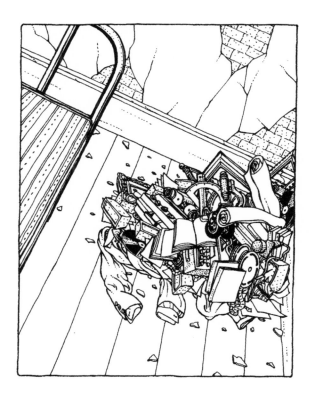

... a faltering swirl a rapidly deteriorating transparent deluge

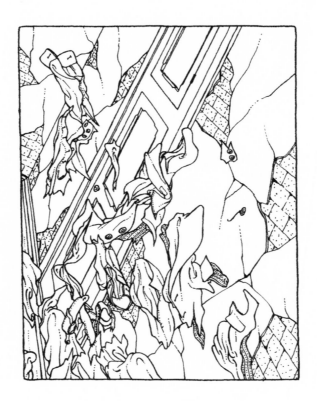

contradictory obstructed by reflections ... an
irrelevant gleaming brittle sheath ...

a frozen geometry of mutilated props a silent drama a wingless crippled and carnivorous repertoire of shrieks...

... the leaves ...

... vegetation ...

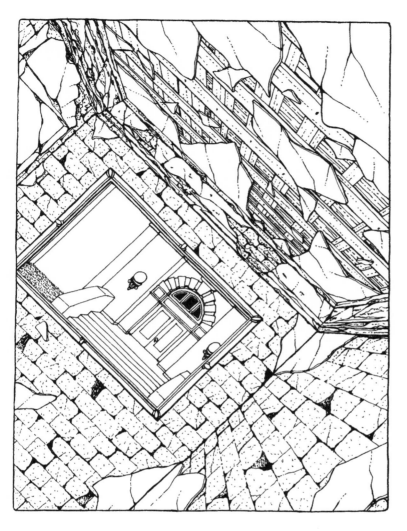

... an ocean of stones ...

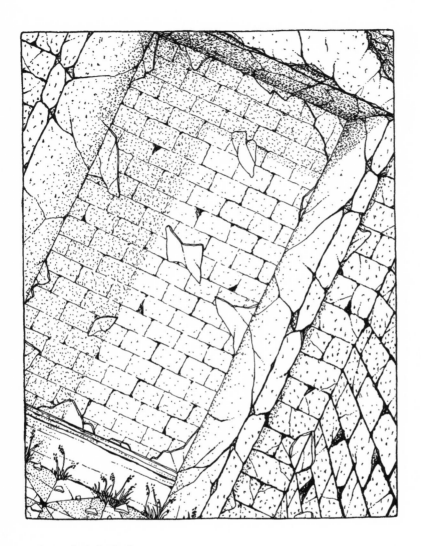

... breath inhaled ...

... and expelled ...

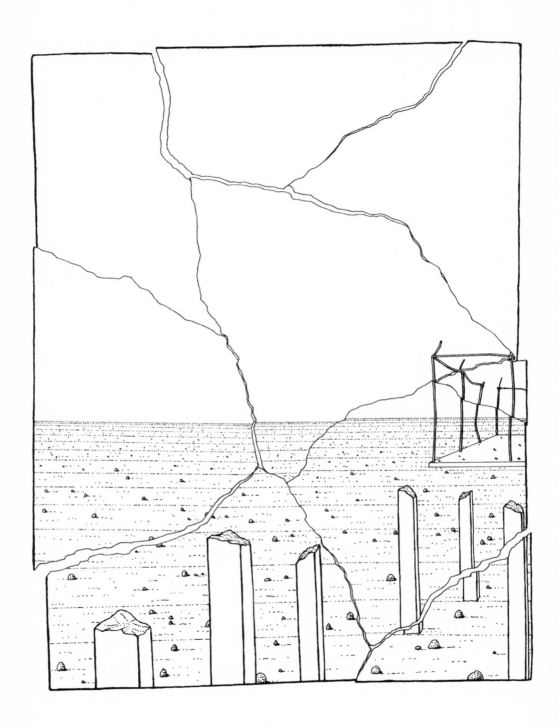

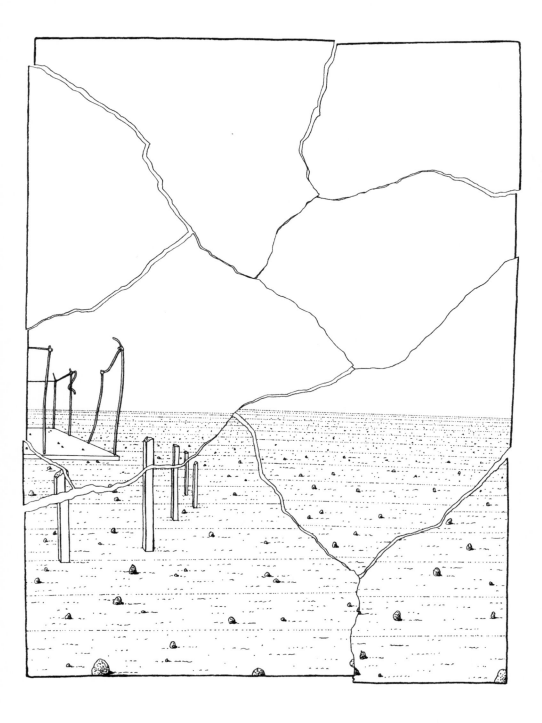

stands as before unfinished and already decayed as if its construction had been abruptly and inexplicably arrested its builders overtaken in their endeavour by some event which for all their skill they had never for an instant anticipated an eruption so sudden and so violent that it reduced to rubble the elaborate structure of which this was merely one feature one facet of a complex network of forms arranged according to some logic separate and alien to the surrounding desolation a labyrinth of distorted signs stretching out across the plain a wild attempt to contain the inevitable flood of mute destruction a string of bloodied rags and broken nails obliterating

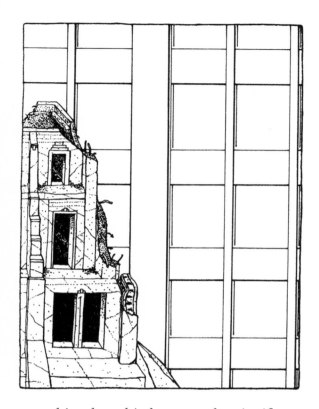

everything but this barren cube significant
only because it remains an empty analogy a
vacuous stale and airless bag of words of
words words words stale airless words
abruptly overtaken by some eruption some
alien logic some event unfinished some barren
bag of broken desolation so violent that it
arrested reduced distorted the elaborate signs
stretching mute across this cube this construction endeavour eruption elaborate structure
network network labyrinth labyrinth labyrinth
labyrinth unfinished and already decayed as if
its construction had been abruptly and inexplicably arrested its builders overtaken in their
endeavour by some event which

The deafening blur of sound is suddenly in focus, crystallized

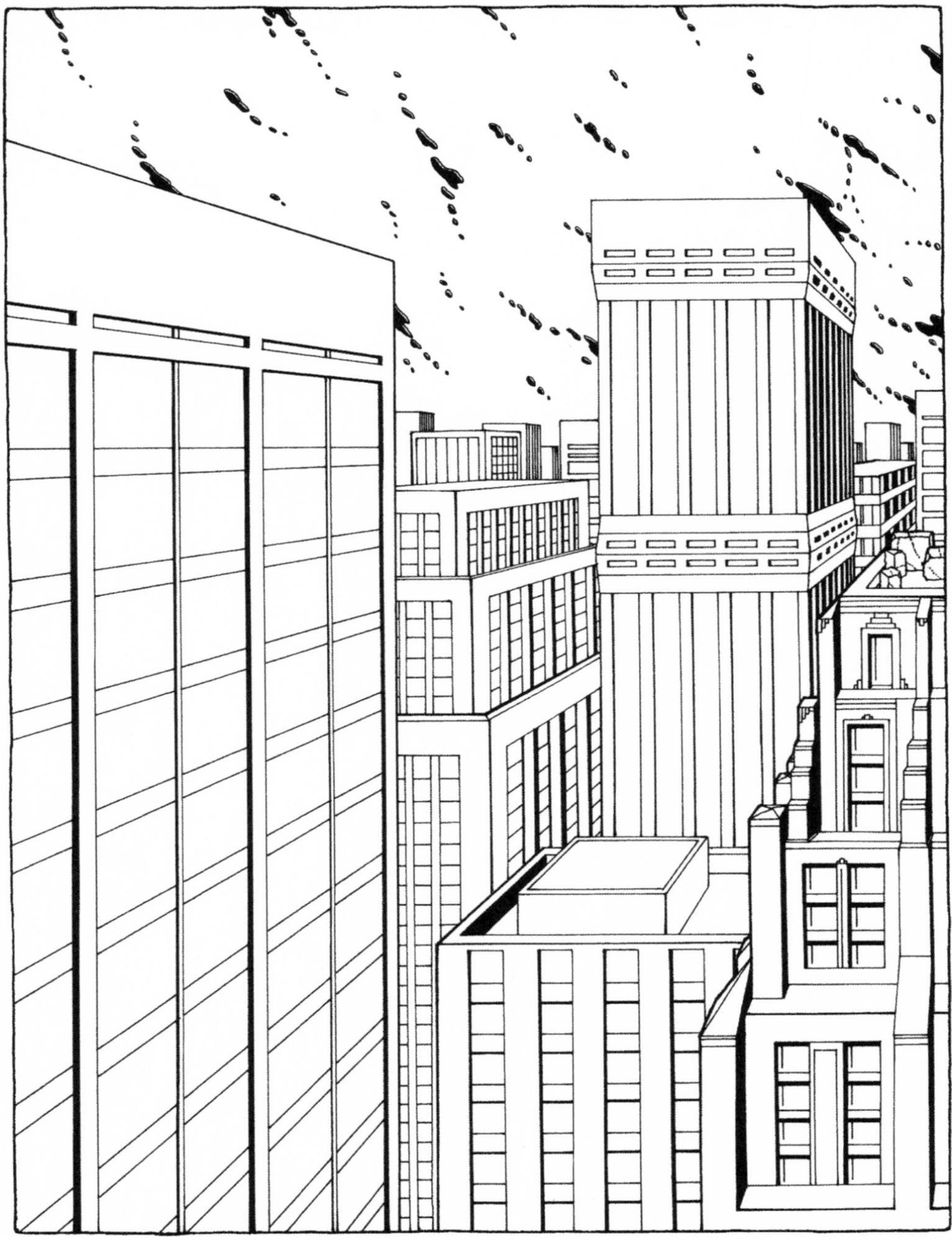

cemented to the screen in unmistakable formations, distinct articulated waves

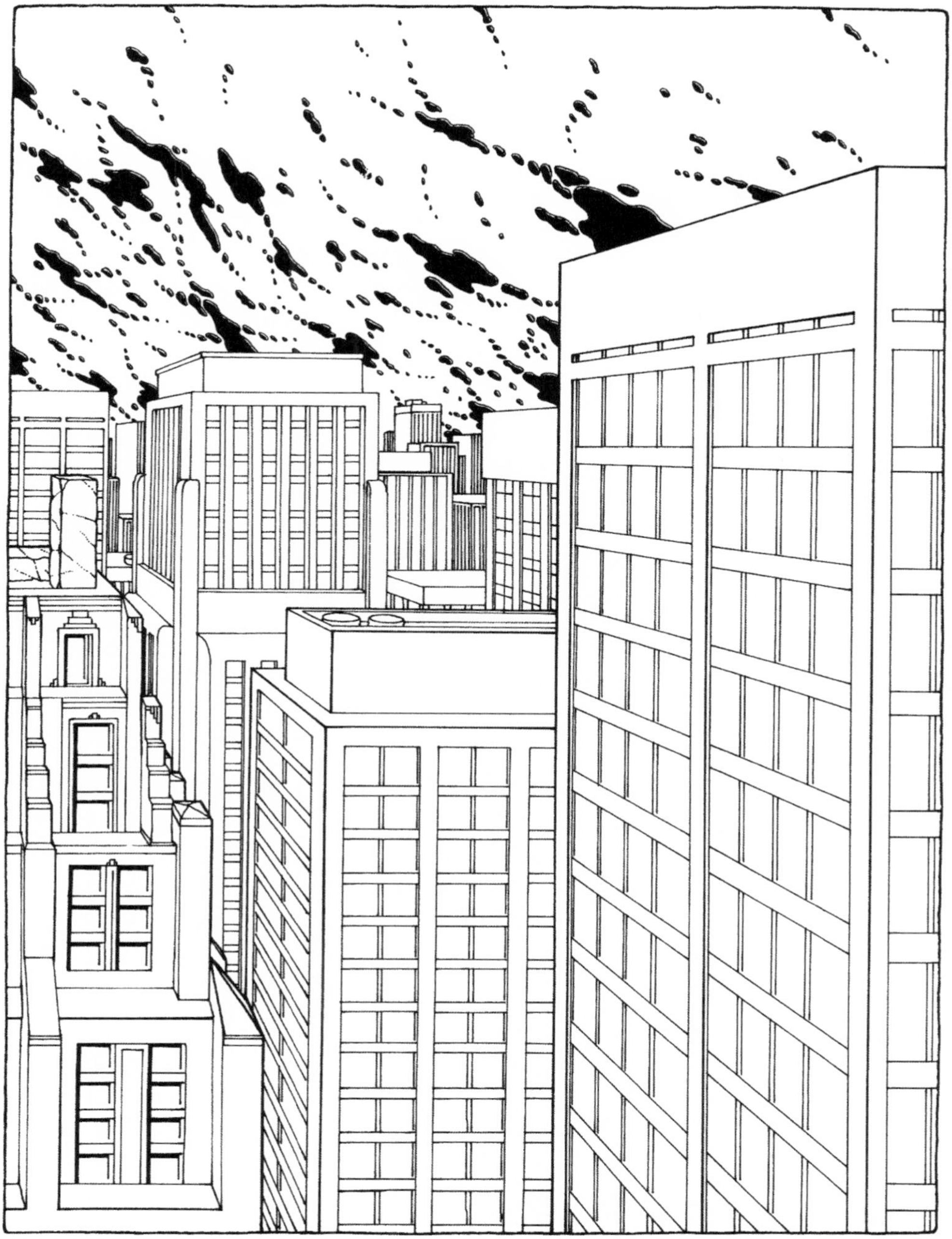

... a multitude of rapid hoarse ejaculations linked in a rhythmic chain ...

a rattling chant deliberately repeated ...

an endless parody of breath gulped in and vomited away ...

an outrageous mimicry of suffocation ... circling with infinite monotony above the ruined plain

above the brief charade now terminating before a mute and sightless audience absorbed as always by all the tedious movements of the machine, all the esoteric variations of each altered revolution of its painted cylinder, all the unpredictable displacements of its contents ... employing blindly all the implements at its disposal in a vain attempt to fix for once and for all time ...

... the ruined plain, rotating on its axis, a galaxy of stones

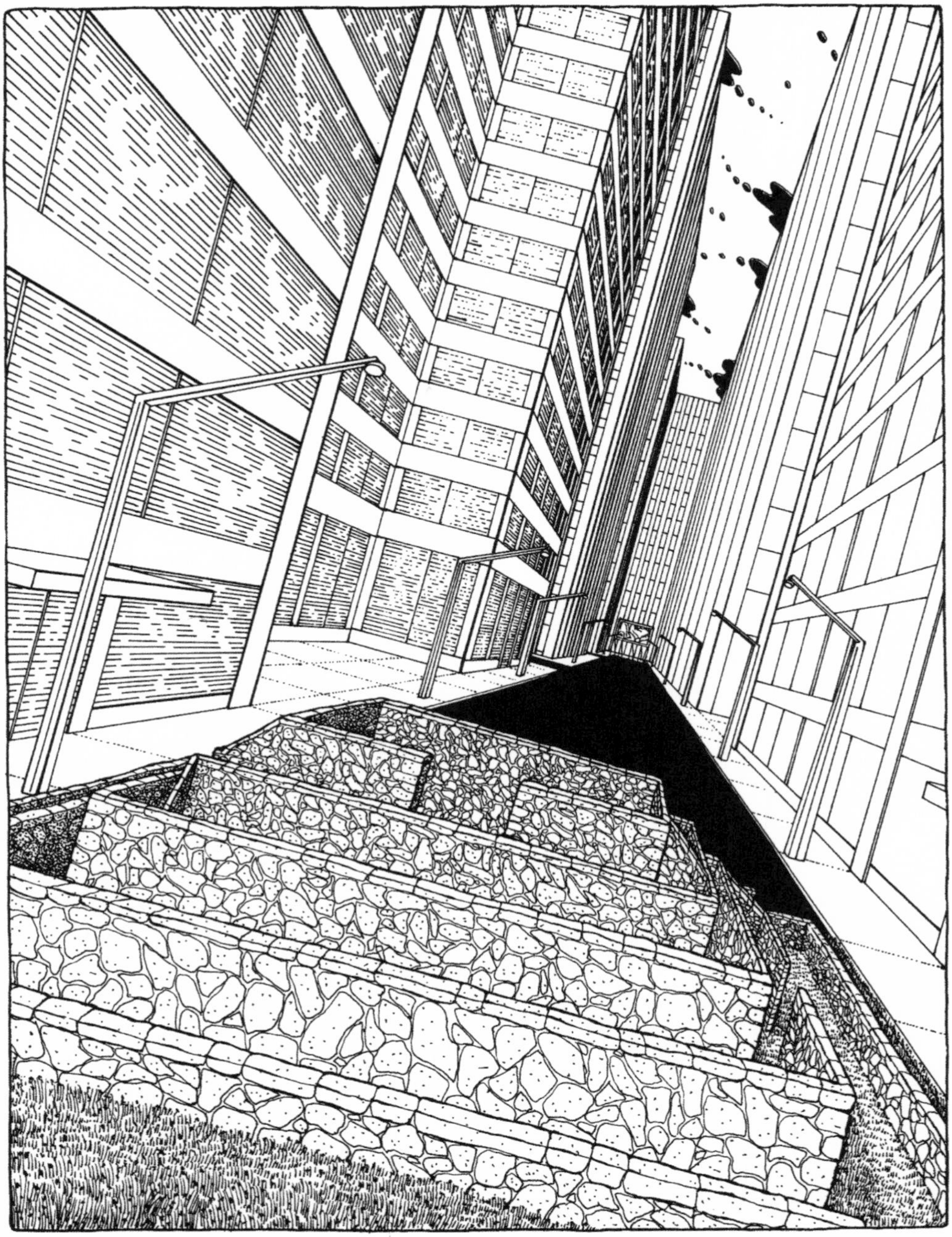

revolving round the pit (a sterile dugout sunk below the horizontal)

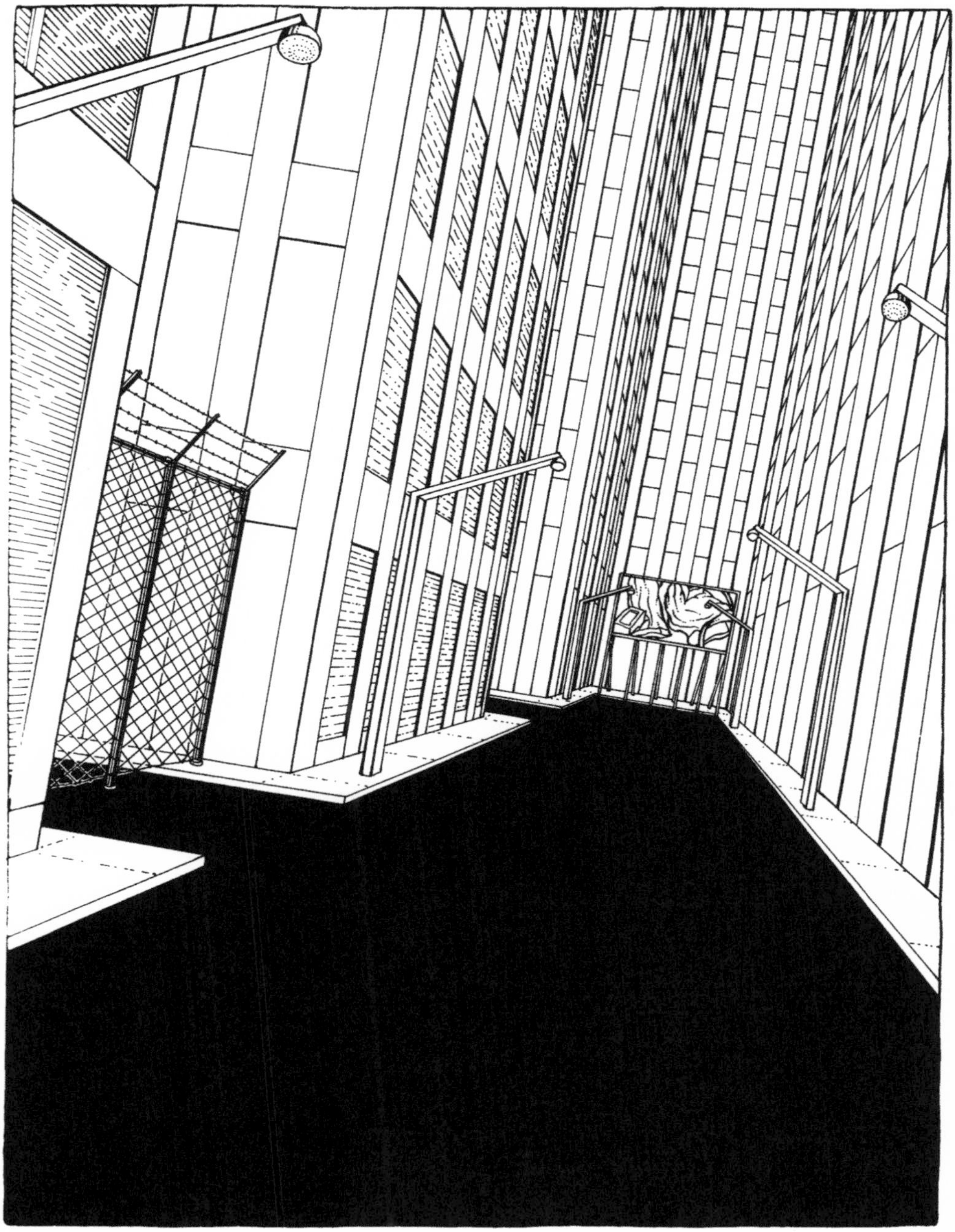

gouged from the frozen bitumen, a massive black receptacle for that still unbuilt construction (its concave geometry buried like a monstrous fossil) now exposed, unearthed an enigmatic crater in the lava of the plain.

The lens probes the darkness at the vortex of the pit, and then withdraws, opening its circle (like a funnel advancing slowly through the oily air) spreading like a stain across the sunken complex until finally contained within the edges of the frame. Here it stops, having reached the full limit of its range.

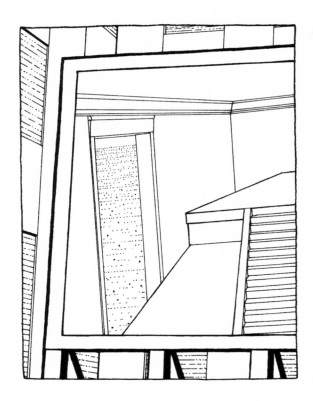

The frame itself, illuminated by the search-lights, hovers (like a spectre) in the darkness ... a phosphorescent image of the archeological desolation, dramatically defaced ... a violent splash cutting right across the centre ... a cross of furious negation ...

a cross whose four distended limbs plough
through each corner of the square and, in
turn, the four concentric trenches until they
meet above the pit.

... a spattered crucifix at whose hysterical
junction is impaled the final artificial insect,
its hollow crippled limbs and brittle wingless
body writhing like a crumpled epileptic above
the chasm of the square.

The first, the shallowest of the trenches, has already gone ...

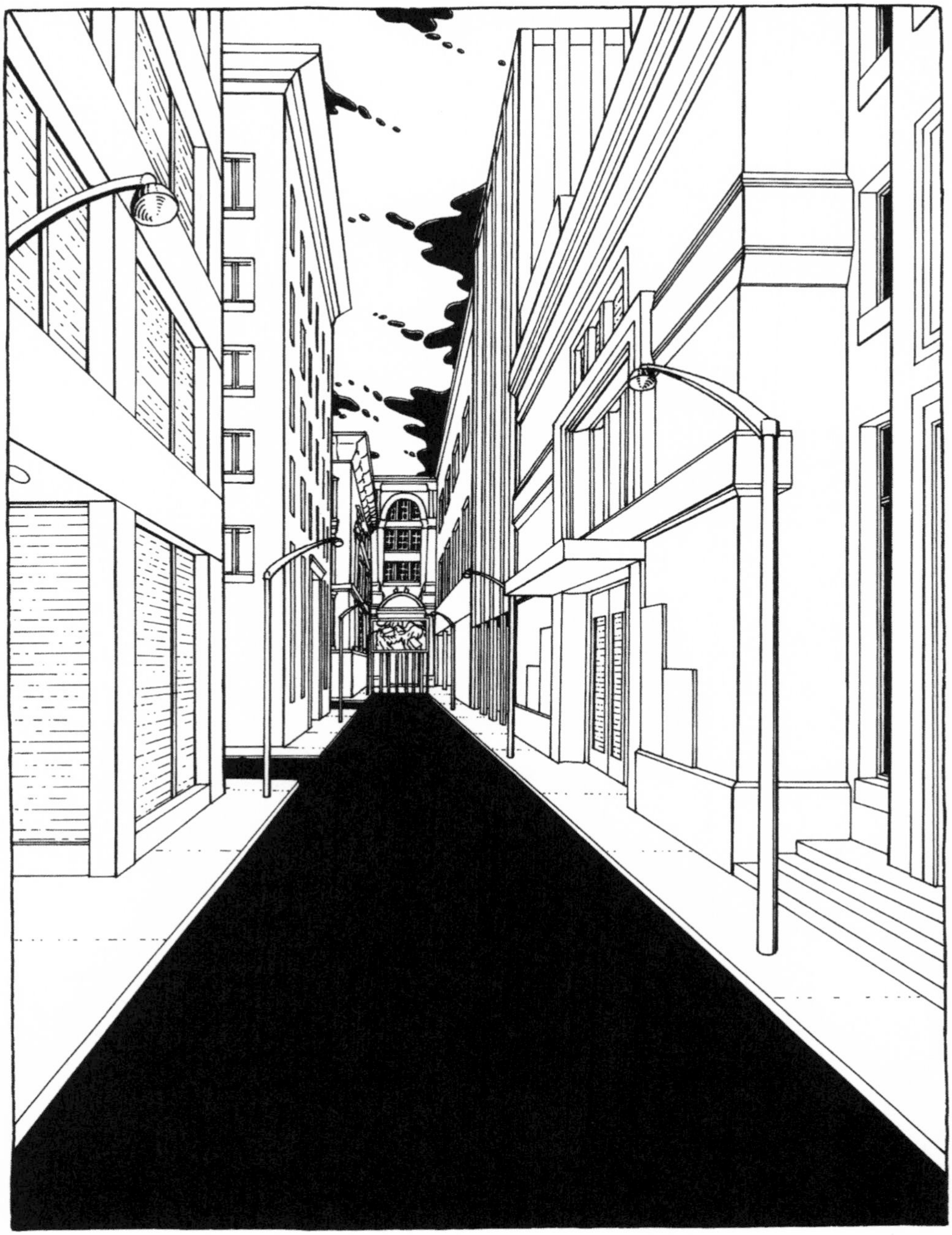

the second, set within its boundaries, is cut deeper, descends more steeply

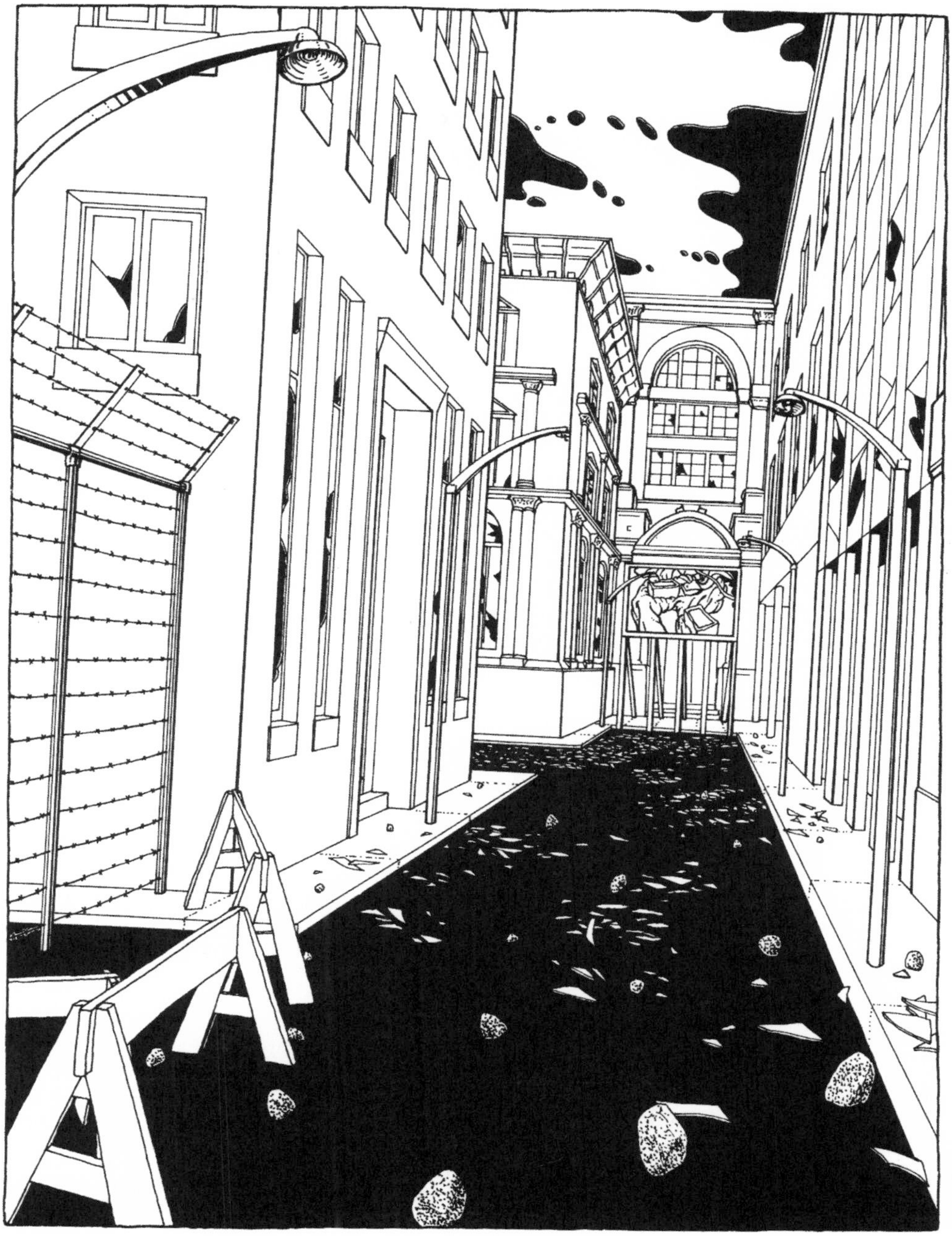

the inky fluid gaining speed as it slides on down this quadri-
lateral spiral, an onyx glacier sweeping before it the broken
debris of previous expeditions, coating like pearls (with the
same black and tepid mucus) the bricks and straps and
metal rods, and leaving in its wake the perennial signs of
imminent collapse ... crumbling plaster, fragmented glass
and flakes of now redundant ornament

... imminent collapse ... hanging like a thin insectoid cross above the pit ... atrophied beneath successive strata of volcanic dirt ... a solid tide of ink ...

... tide rolling head on against the sunken
wall, swelling in a gleaming arc, doubling
back and crumpling on itself, and, having
nowhere else to run, veering like a panicked
animal to the left, always to the left, back
toward that magnetic centre, the vanguard of
the flood forced on by the sheer momentum
of its weight ... plunging blindly off this
second parapet and sweeping on ...

... forced by blind momentum, an avalanche
of signs and emblems devouring the stone ...
insane graffiti blistering across the walls like
a plague of putrid fungi ...
the room, that ultimate enclosure, cut adrift
and spewed out through the tunnel ...

... plunging blindly back toward that magnetic centre ...

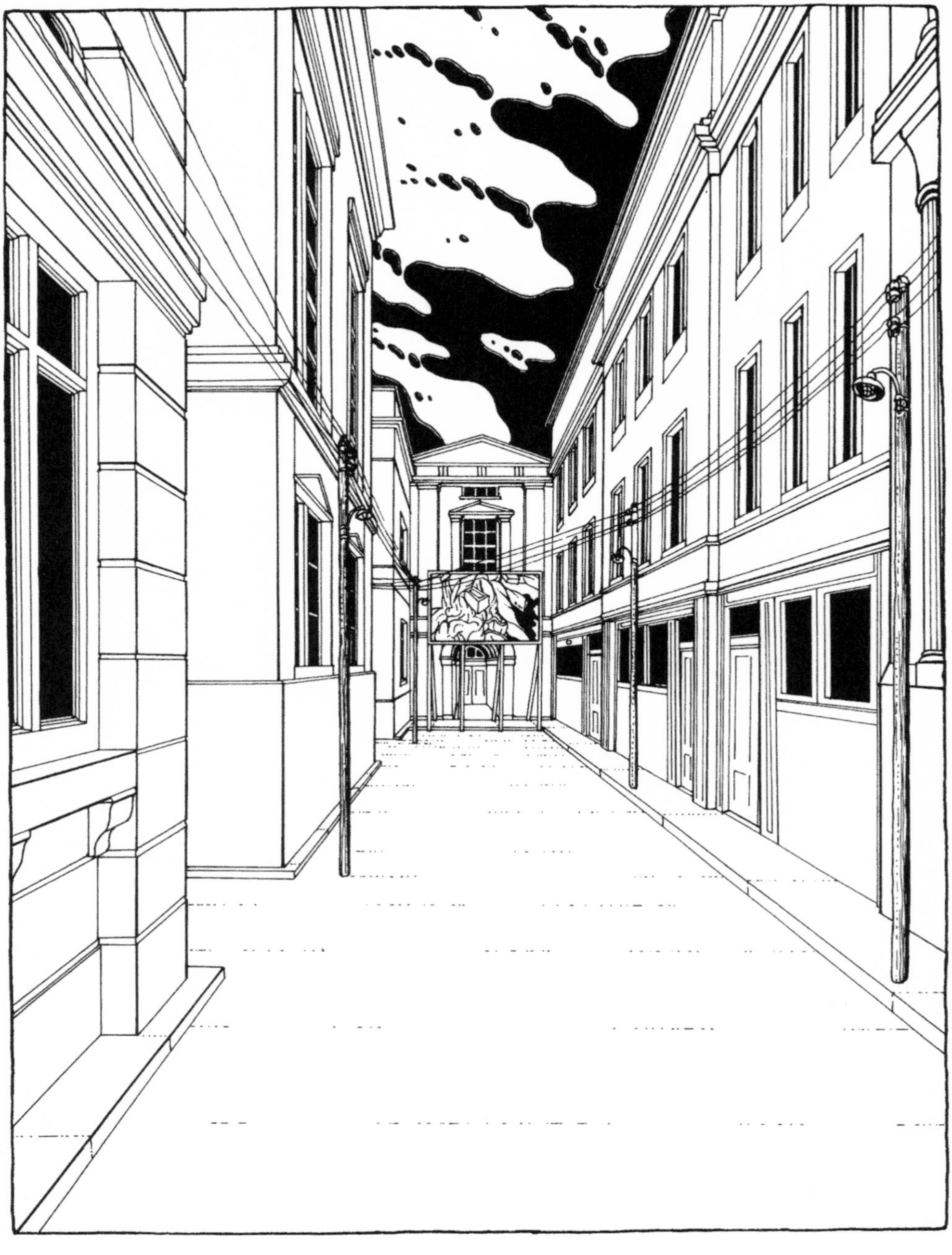

hypnotic tomb ... ... leaving in its wake ...

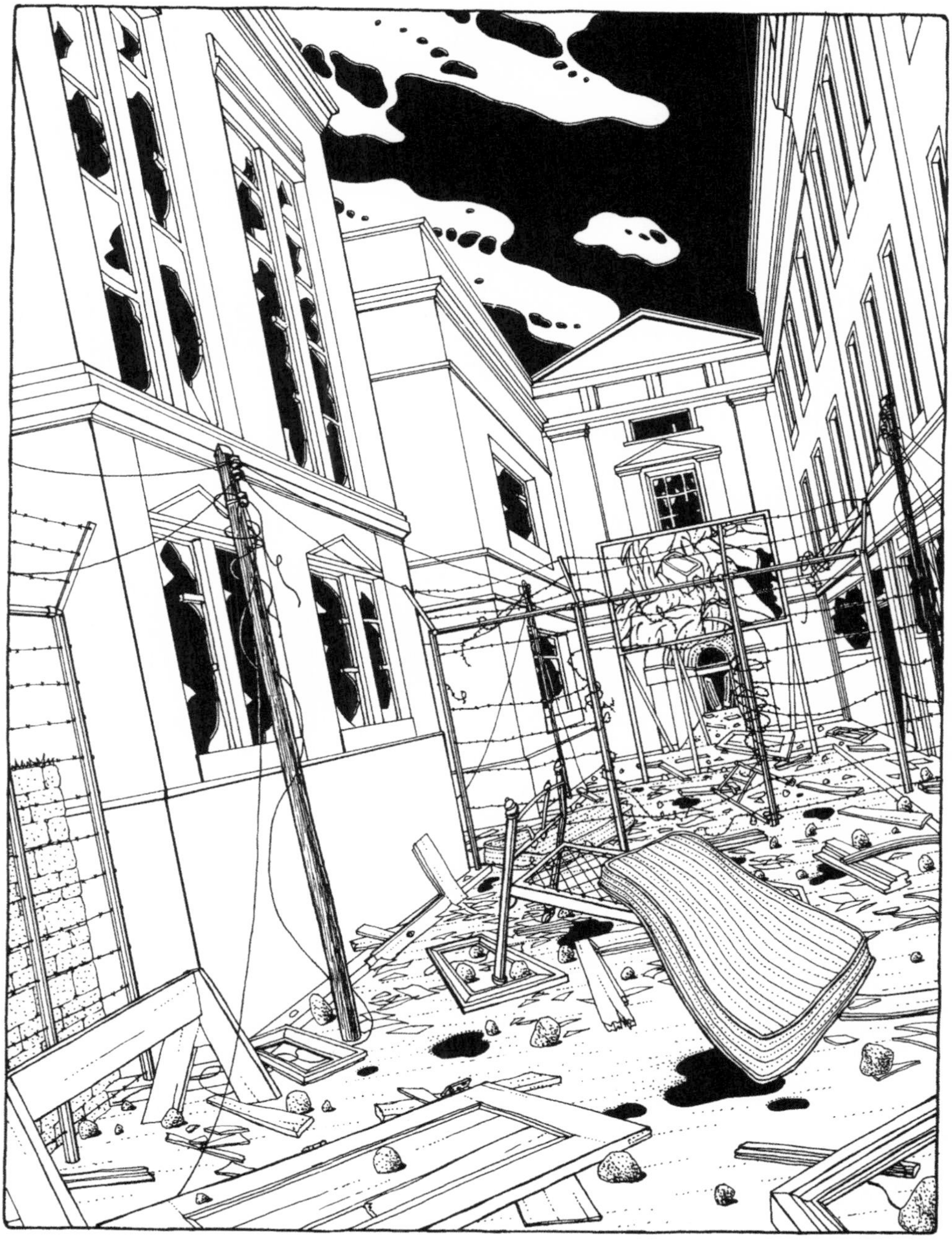

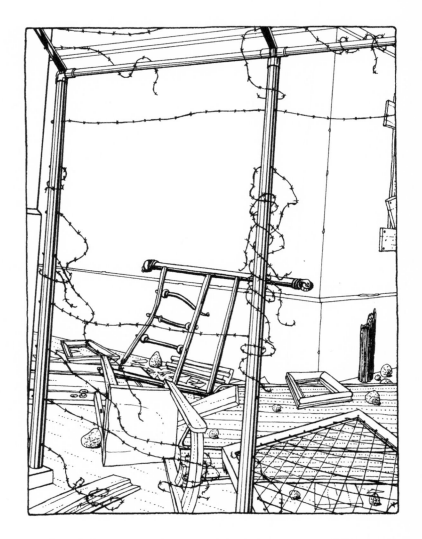

... the plain ... paved across its vast expanse with stones, sweeping like a cobbled sea beneath that line, that perfect horizontal drawn across the void ... an arid, inorganic residue, stretching out toward a single, hard, remote and unassailable frontier ... the sky ... as white as paper ... standing on its end, a cliff of ice encasing like debris within a glacier, a bank of clouds ... stratified and motionless ... extinct ...

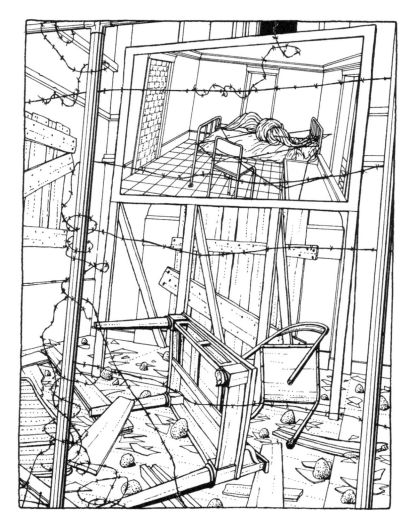

a solid swamp of inbred malformations ... a shrivelled ocean in retreat ... the posts ... winding like a row of faceless dolmens ... blank, unmarked, as if all inscriptions had been removed or worn away or had been void from the beginning, vacant incapable of bearing any sign except a brutal splash, as if their mere presence trailing out toward the mound would in all events suffice ...

their virgin masks ... perpetual grimaces splitting imperceptibly through every shell ... buried or unearthed ... approached through ruins flanked by rows of black and bloated implements ... cast down upon the threshold of the stair and hacked to pieces ... flayed, knotted ... shattered into fragments and dispersed ... settling like ash, layer upon layer, gently blotting out, submerging, drawing down the few remaining pillars of this crumbling facade... a quiet and inevitable inundation ...

a field of mud congealing in the corridors ... a vast configuration of decaying rags and rusted skewers ... an excrement of beds and picture frames and ossified machinery ... clotted rope and canvas, swollen clumps of bedding, rods and pedestals ... rubble ... compost ... seeping into every pore and crevice ... penetrating every subterranean recess until totally absorbed ... solidifying so that they became one grotesque and indivisible mélange ... the sterile flood and the impregnated plain.

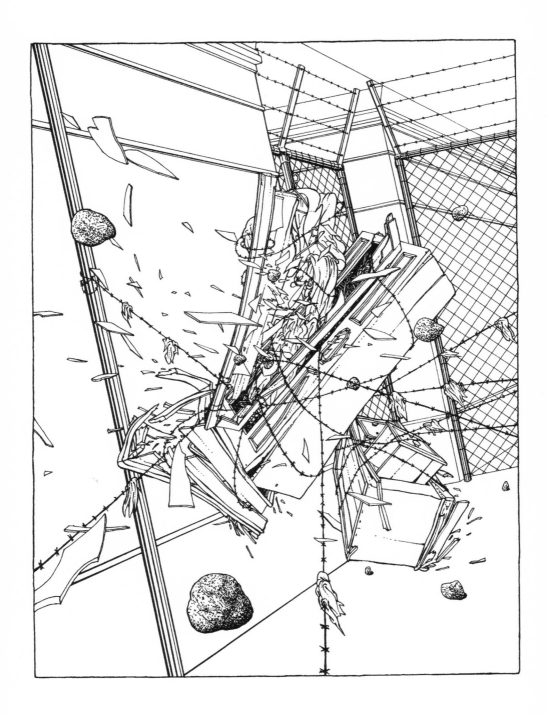

... plummeting like a siren screaming down the well ...

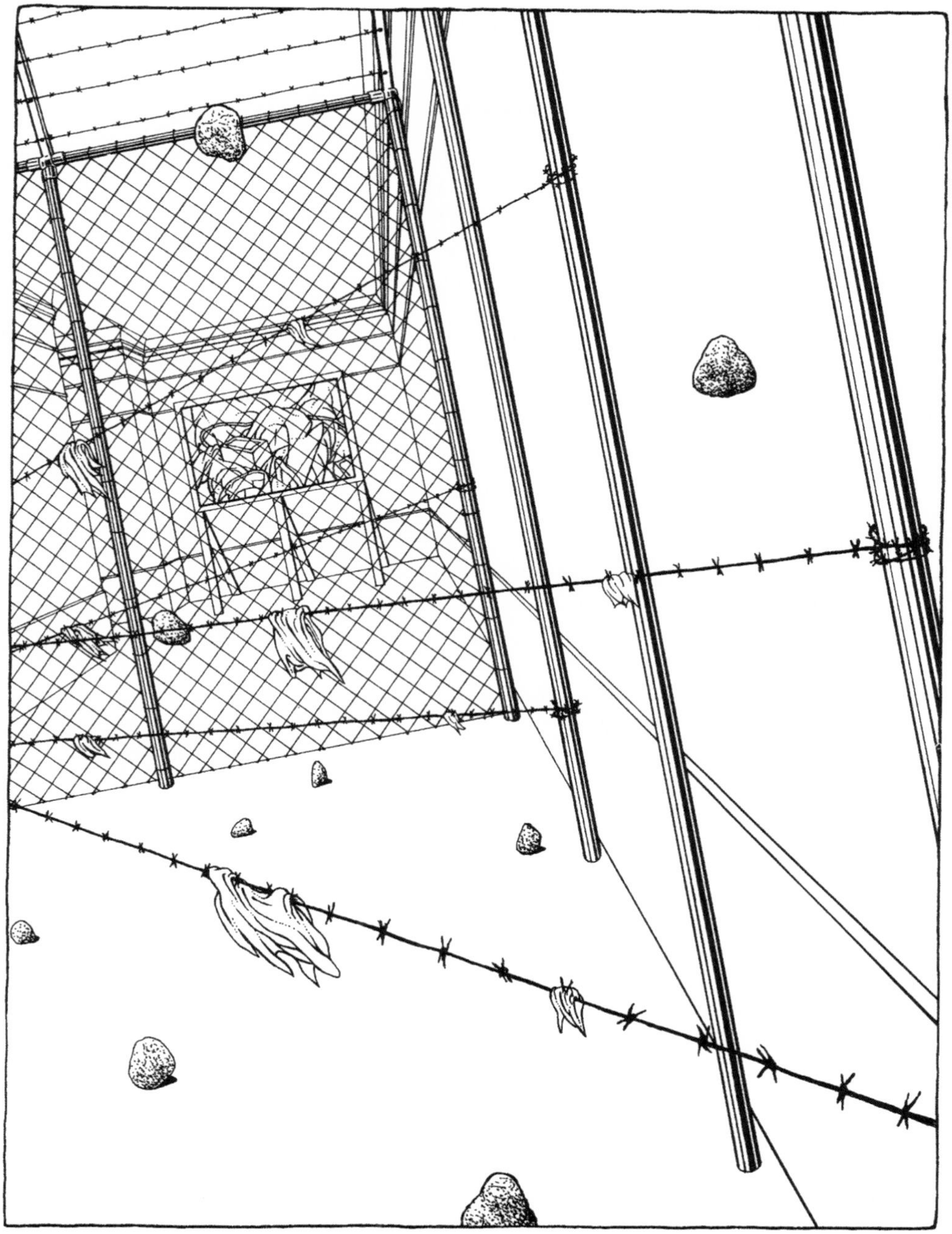

... the room choking on its rancid cube of air, dismembered by the spastic acrobatics of the machine, the skewered whirlpool at its core, the blurred and ruptured cylinder ...

its stricken contents glued against its melting wall, clawing frantically to free from all the stinking painted refuse that thing still clinging to the centre of the pit ...

... the cage, the cage, the cage, the cage, the cage ...

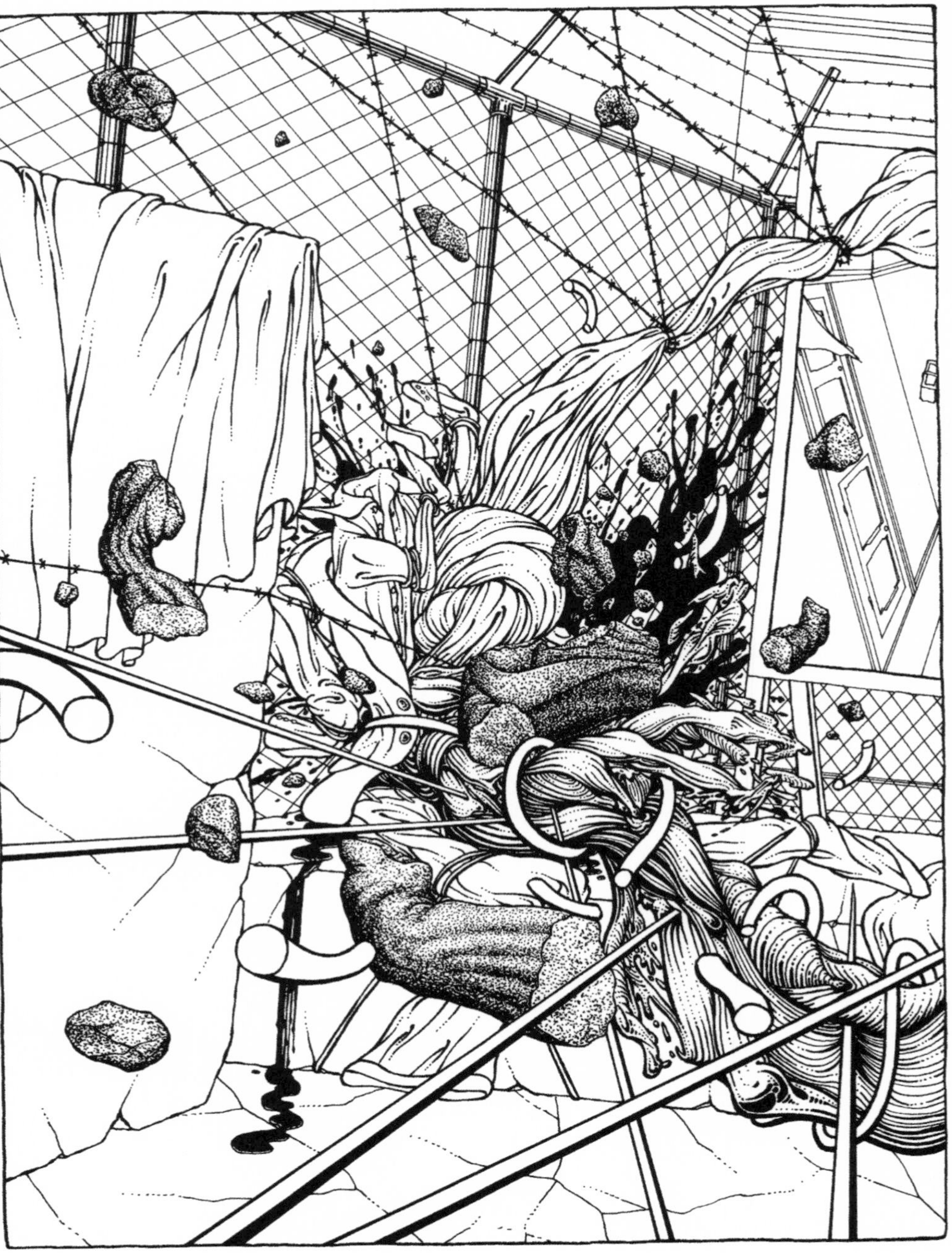

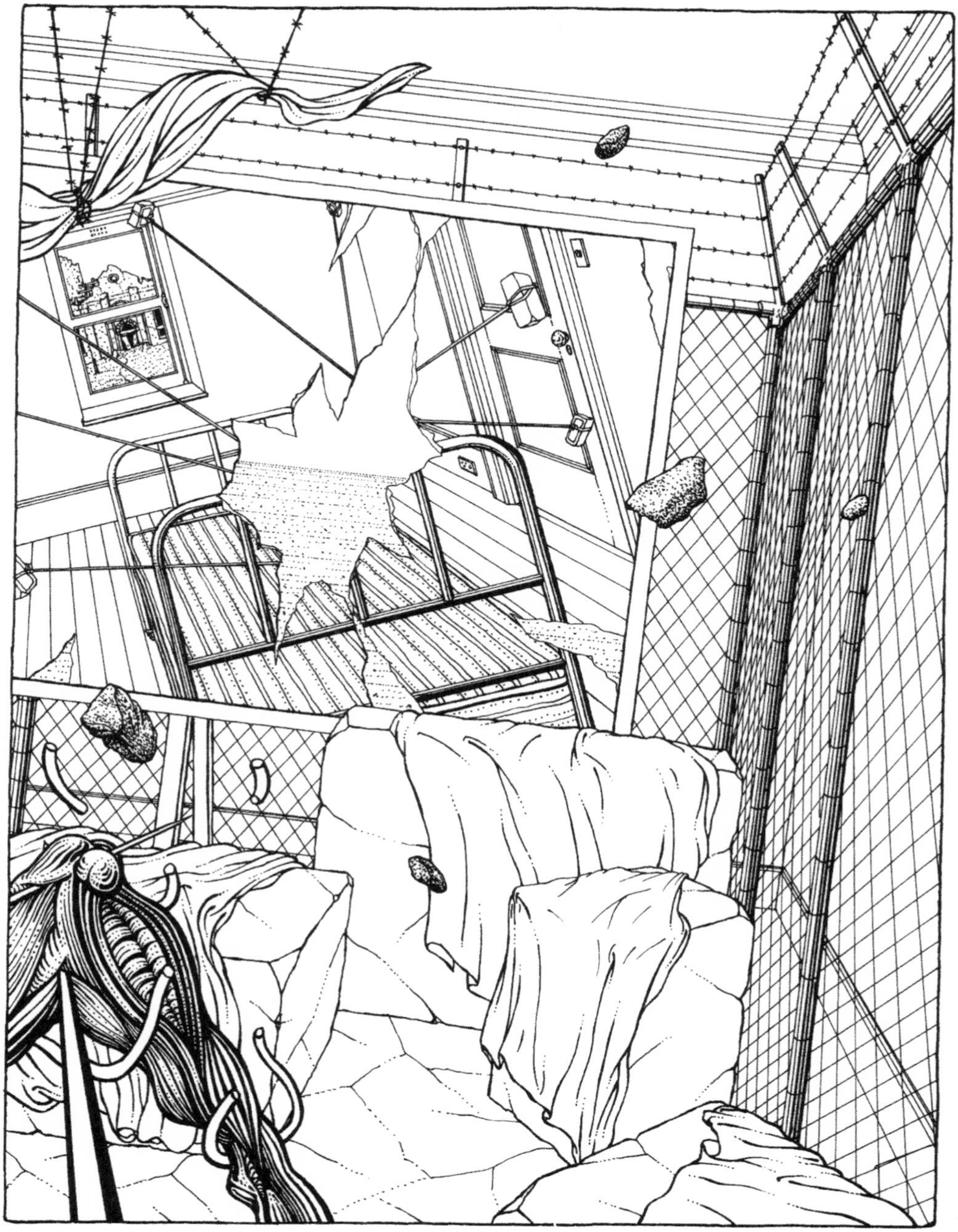

the cage ...

... the cage ...

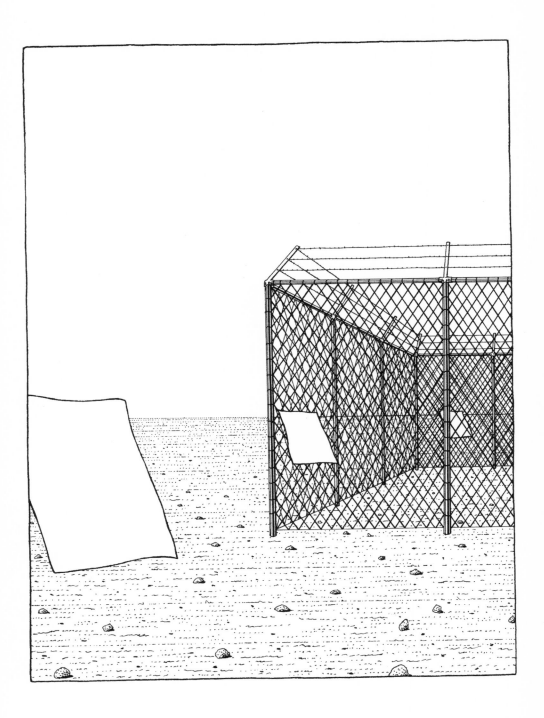

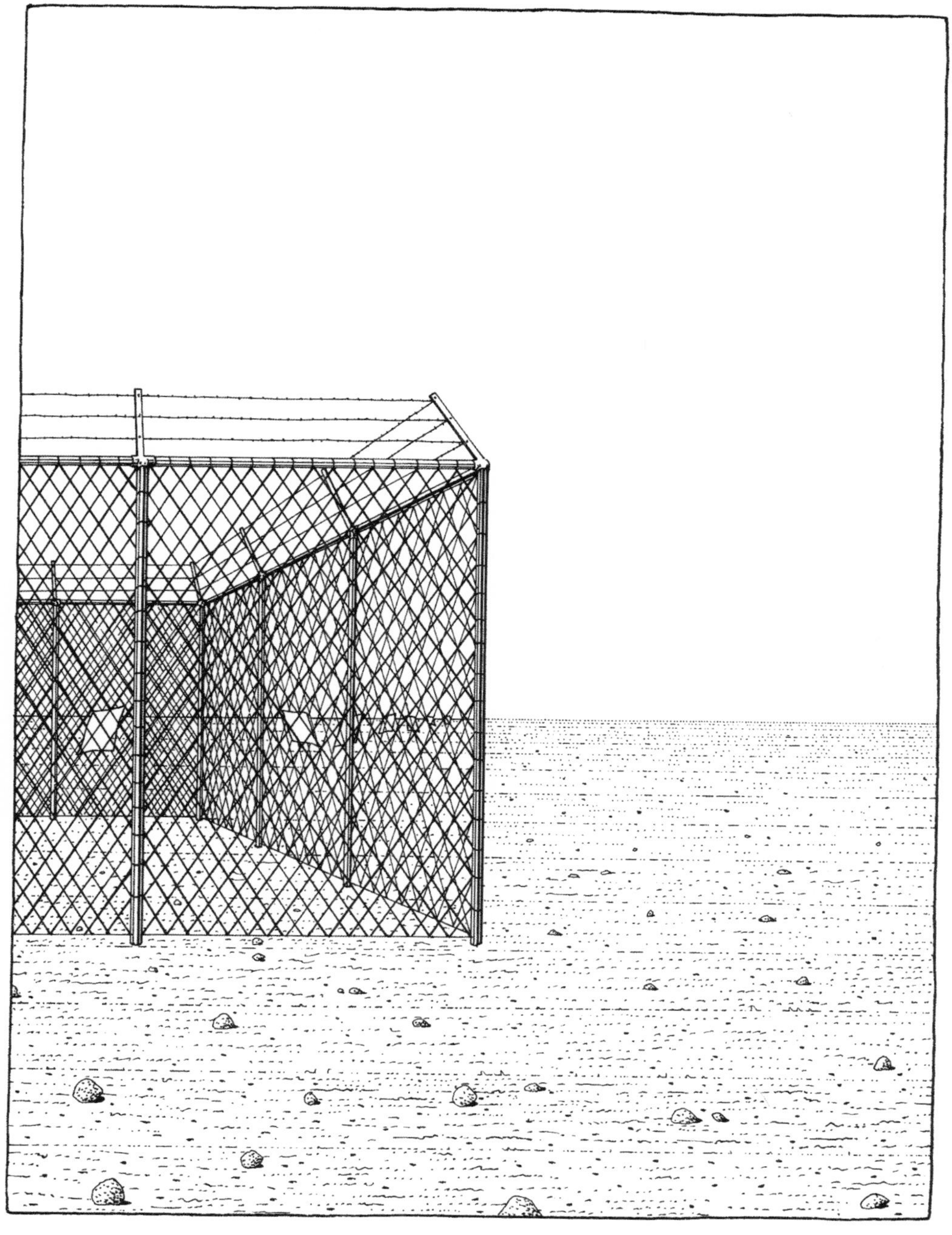

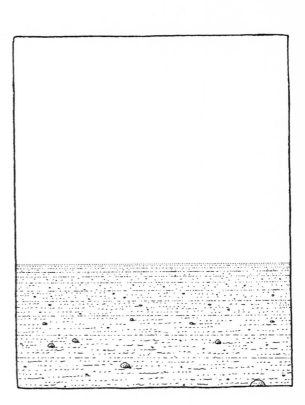

Typeset in Goluska, designed by Canadian Rod McDonald to honour his longtime friend Glenn Goluska (1947– 2011). Goluska was one of Canada's finest designers, who had a life-long love for the work of noted American typographer William Addison Dwiggins. The typeface Goluska is an homage to the Dwiggins' font, Electra.

Assembled and bound at the old Coach House on bpNichol Lane in Toronto, Ontario.
Cover and design by Rick/Simon
Photo of Martin in 1975 by Sarah McCoy
Martin Vaughn-James self portrait, page 11

ABOUT THE AUTHOR

Martin Vaughn-James (1943–2009) was a painter and groundbreaking comics artist who published four graphic novels: *Elephant* (1970), *The Projector* (1971), *The Park* (1972) and *The Cage* (1975). Born in England, he spent much of his youth in Australia before moving to Canada. Vaughn-James is widely recognized as a pioneer in the development of the graphic novel. Later in life, he moved to Belgium, where he focused on painting. Vaughn-James also published two works of prose fiction: *Night Train* (1989) and *The Tomb of Zwaab* (1991).

M.V-J. 1975

Coach House Books
80 bpNichol Lane
Toronto, ON M5S 3J4
Canada

416 979 2217
800 367 6360

mail@chbooks.com
www.chbooks.com